"No American alive today has s
lation growth. This reality seei   MW01028670   ....g church
planting our way. J. D. points back to the simple biblical cycle designed to
multiply. Grasping this cycle demands we wrestle with serious questions: Can
new churches be formed from new believers? Can new pastors develop and
emerge from within new churches? Can faithful church planting include an
exit to leave new churches to develop on their own? J. D. Payne not only
defends the potential of such notions, he demonstrates the biblical *expectation*
that church planting be done this way."

Nathan Shank, church planting catalyst in Asia,
coauthor of *The Four Fields of Kingdom Growth*

"Church planting is not a new concept to many, even in North America.
However, the idea of apostolic church planting will be new and novel to many.
The idea of teams who start with evangelism, allow those they reach to
become a body of believers, focus on growing leaders and do all of this with
an eye to leaving represents an old-new idea—old as the New Testament, new
to us. In a nation that is increasingly hostile to the things of Christ, J. D.'s
work is a much-needed call back to a biblical pattern of seeing the church
take root among people who do not know him. If you are looking for biblical
and practical help in how to mobilize teams of people for church planting,
this book is a wonderful resource."

Van Kicklighter, associate executive director, church planting team,
Illinois Baptist State Association

"In this excellent work, J. D. Payne draws from his experience as a practitioner
in the roles of church planter, sponsoring church mission pastor and planter
coach to provide timely wisdom for those who are about to begin or are already traversing the church planting journey. Writing as a practitioner, his
insights are practical and relevant. As a leading missiologist, his wisdom is
well-grounded and trustworthy. In this book, Payne addresses some specific
issues not covered in his earlier book, *Discovering Church Planting*. These two
books should be tattered from use, highlighted, dog-eared and at the fin-
gertips of every person leading any church planting endeavor."

Mark Custalow, church planting strategist, central east and southeast Virginia,
Southern Baptist Conservatives of Virginia

"In a concise and readable manner, J. D. Payne has written a foundational book
for church planters. Whether ministering in North America or around the

globe, this is a must-read for anyone who is called to plant churches. For veteran church planters, it could serve as a useful reminder of, and perhaps as an encouragement to recalibrate, the principles of their church-planting ministry."

James Kim, executive director, Pioneers Canada

"Church planting must always be grounded in evangelism—reaching people who are not yet Christians with the gospel. When church planting degenerates into gathering disaffected Christians or otherwise reshuffling the already-converted into new congregational forms, it really isn't church planting at all! This book clearly articulates a model of true church planting and calls us to fulfill its biblical mandate. Read it and be challenged!"

Jeff Iorg, president, Golden Gate Seminary

"Many church planters who would say they follow the apostles' methods fail to see churches multiply as the apostles did. They *must* read J. D. Payne's *Apostolic Church Planting*! He graciously points out the shortcomings of conventional church plants in a way that does not appear 'anti,' untying the usual knotty problems and simplifying common complications. I love his phrase, 'Plant the church that is, not the church to come.' Had I read that when I was young, I'd have avoided years of foolishly trying to birth mature churches! You will find these gems throughout the book, but brace yourself to face challenges from Scripture, field experience and testimonies of a healthy number of highly effective practitioners."

George Patterson, church multiplier, author of *Church Multiplication Guide*, *Come Quickly Dawn* and *Train and Multiply*

"J. D. Payne strategically shows how sustainable and sanctified apostolic church planting (churches birthed from disciple making) is actually simple, and he skillfully does so without being simplistic."

Tom Steffen, emeritus professor of intercultural studies, Cook School of Intercultural Studies, Biola University

"*Apostolic Church Planting* is less like a how-to manual and more like a clinician's guidebook. It deals with the theology and theory of church planting as well as the practical steps involved. Few missiologists could have written it, but J. D. Payne is one of them. All who are in any way involved in church planting should study this book to be informed. All should read it to be refreshed."

David J. Hesselgrave, professor emeritus of mission, Trinity Evangelical Divinity School

APOSTOLIC CHURCH PLANTING

BIRTHING NEW CHURCHES FROM NEW BELIEVERS

•••

J. D. PAYNE

IVP Books

An imprint of InterVarsity Press
Downers Grove, Illinois

InterVarsity Press
P.O. Box 1400, Downers Grove, IL 60515-1426
ivpress.com
email@ivpress.com

InterVarsity Press® is the book-publishing division of InterVarsity Christian Fellowship/USA®, a movement of students and faculty active on campus at hundreds of universities, colleges and schools of nursing in the United States of America, and a member movement of the International Fellowship of Evangelical Students. For information about local and regional activities, visit intervarsity.org.

Scripture quotations, unless otherwise noted, are from The Holy Bible, English Standard Version, copyright © 2001 by Crossway Bibles, a division of Good News Publishers. Used by permission. All rights reserved.

While any stories in this book are true, some names and identifying information may have been changed to protect the privacy of individuals.

Cover design: Cindy Kiple
Interior design: Beth McGill
Images: planet with people: ©johavel/iStockphoto

ISBN 978-0-8308-4124-0 (print)
ISBN 978-0-8308-9890-9 (digital)

Printed in the United States of America ∞

Library of Congress Cataloging-in-Publication Data
Payne, Jervis David, 1974-
Apostolic church planting : birthing new churches from new believers / J.D. Payne.
    pages cm
Includes bibliographical references.
    ISBN 978-0-8308-4124-0 (pbk. : alk. paper)
1. Church development, New. 2. Discipling (Christianity) I. Title.
BV652.24.P388 2015
254'.1—dc23

                                                                    2015027567

P   21   20   19   18   17   16   15   14   13   12   11   10   9   8   7   6   5   4

Y   33   32   31   30   29   28   27   26   25   24   23   22   21   20   19

To my heavenly Father

and my earthly partner, Sarah

• • •

Contents

Preface

●●●

When I wrote *Discovering Church Planting: An Introduction to the Whats, Whys, and Hows of Global Church Planting*, I wanted to provide a comprehensive guide on the topic.[1] That book is almost 460 pages long, and I believe I accomplished what the Lord placed in my heart. I am very thankful and pleased with that book.

You might assume that such a book was adequately thorough. However, over years of training church planters in both seminaries and local churches, I have often encountered questions I did not address in *Discovering Church Planting*. Also, since it was an introductory text, space and purpose would not allow me to develop some of my thinking to the degree that I would have liked.

The book you have before you, *Apostolic Church Planting*, is my attempt to respond to some of those questions and to connect the practical steps in a more developed manner. While this book is written to stand on its own, with much new material, it is also written to complement—not replace—*Discovering Church Planting*. Naturally, there is some overlap between the two. If there weren't, you would be wise to question an author who writes two books on a subject with no continuity and much divergence in thought.

However, there are very important matters related to church planting that I do not address in detail in this book but do in

Discovering Church Planting. This book says little about the role of the Holy Spirit, fasting and prayer, spiritual warfare and the role of the sending church. While these vital aspects of missionary labors are not completely absent from this book, I intentionally avoid being redundant and instead direct the reader to respective chapters in *Discovering Church Planting* for additional reading. It is my hope that *Apostolic Church Planting* will not be read as lacking discussion of important matters for the multiplication of disciples, leaders and churches. Rather, I hope you will recognize that this book is part of the larger context of material I have produced.

There is nothing new under the sun. Every author is influenced by men and women who have gone before, and their writings reflect that. My work is no different. For those of you familiar with the literature of church planting and missiology, you will recognize the influence of Roland Allen, Donald McGavran and Ralph Winter. Among others, you will encounter David Hesselgrave's influence on my thinking regarding the Church Multiplication Cycle, and Tom Steffen and Nathan and Kari Shank when it comes to role changes, stages of church planting and phase-out.[2]

Just before writing this preface, I pulled Charles Brock's *Indigenous Church Planting: A Practical Journey* from my shelf and read where Charles signed his book for me on June 3, 1996, with the words, "May God bless you—Charles Brock."[3] I was introduced to both Charles and his book that summer, and it was through this brother and his writing that the Lord brought me into the world of church planting. In addition to working with church-planting teams in the United States, I've spent ten years teaching church planting in a seminary context. Presently, I serve as the pastor of church multiplication with The Church at Brook Hills in Birmingham, Alabama. One of my responsibilities is to equip our members to serve on church-planting teams. Had Charles

Brock not taught a church-planting course in June 1996, I doubt that I would have written this book. And if you are familiar with Charles's writing, you will recognize his influence on this book in more ways than one.

It is my prayer that the Lord will use *Apostolic Church Planting* to lead you and your team to multiply disciples, leaders and churches among the unreached peoples of the world. A day is coming when such labors will no longer be necessary. I hope you will be part of contributing to that diverse gathering around the throne (Rev 7:9), and I greatly desire that in some small way, this book will assist you in that grand endeavor.

Introduction

•••

One day I met with a seasoned church-planting strategist at a local coffee shop. This wonderful brother had been involved in church planting for many years. Early in our conversation he asked me about my approach to church planting and what our church was doing in the area. I began by defining church planting as evangelism that results in new churches. Then, for the next several minutes, I reflected on some passages of Scripture (such as Acts 13–14; 20; 1 Tim 3; Tit 1), different stages of church planting, planned role changes for the church-planting team and the priority of unreached people groups. After sharing, I waited for his response.

There was a pause as he stared at me. Then, with a look of surprise, he burst out, "Wow! That's amazing!"

He was shocked.

Like anyone else, I love to be commended on a job well done, and I especially enjoy it when someone compliments my innovative idea, action, book or so on. But his response was not encouraging to me. Even though his surprise revealed that he thought I was creative and innovative, I was troubled.

I had described to him nothing more than what we read about in Scripture. It was at that moment that I concluded: *when the*

Church is shocked at a biblical model, it reveals just how far away from the Scriptures we have moved in our missionary practices.

Once, speaking at a church-planting conference, I gave a presentation similar to what I had shared in the coffee shop that day. Afterward a church-planting leader for his denomination came up to me immediately, declaring, "That's exactly what we are doing! Evangelism that results in new churches!"

"Keep up the great work," I replied. However, his declaration did not match what I knew to be true of the church planters he oversaw.

At another speaking engagement addressing the topic of church planting, I had a church-planting strategist approach me and say the same thing: "That's exactly what we're doing! Evangelism that results in new churches!"

"Keep up the great work," I replied again. But again, his statement did not reflect his reality. This time, I was even more familiar with the area he was overseeing.

It is one thing to be sincere and to want something good; it is another matter to act on those emotions.

What I will describe in this book is nothing new. Yes, I have obviously crafted this book according to my own convictions. But apostolic church planting has been with the Church for two thousand years. It is my desire that churches, networks, denominations and mission agencies recognize this matter and respond appropriately. Many western evangelical structures, organizations, training paradigms and support systems will have to change significantly in order to embrace an apostolic approach to church planting.

Many think they have already embraced this approach; reality shouts otherwise.

Change is never easy. It is not my purpose in this book to address such necessary changes. However, evangelicals must begin to make necessary adjustments as we continue into the twenty-first century. Over six thousand people groups remain unreached (including three thousand unengaged-unreached). More of the same is not sufficient. While great things have been accomplished for the kingdom in the realm of church planting, we must build on them and venture into new waters with an ancient approach.

Apostolic church planting provides a path to the nations. If it surprises us, we should ask, "Why?"

If what kingdom stewards should expect excites us, we should reevaluate our convictions, methods, strategies, systems and structures.

If our present realities do not match such expectations, something must change.

A day is coming when disciple-making and church-planting efforts will cease to exist. Until that time, we are called to be wise stewards with what we have received—laboring for the completion of the multiethnic multitude gathered around the throne (Rev 7:9). Will you join in this divine task with Jesus, building his church? Will you embrace apostolic church planting as a means for making disciples of all peoples—across the street and around the world?

one

What Is Church Planting?

•••

Many people have an interest in the topic of church planting. Books, articles and websites abound on the topic. Churches, networks, agencies and entire denominations are interested in church planting. Across the world, the church is talking about church planting. There are whole conferences on this topic. Seminaries offer courses on the subject. Some schools offer degrees in church planting. Church planting is here, there and everywhere! And this is a good thing.

Yet here is a fascinating fact: nowhere in the Bible is the church commanded to plant churches. No such reference exists. Certainly, we find church planting taking place, but that is a different matter than a direct command. We are commanded to make disciples (Mt 28:19). This Great Commission involves baptizing and teaching (Mt 28:19-20). And the context in which disciples are to follow Christ and experience sanctification is local kingdom communities—local churches.

But the Bible does not tell us to plant churches.

Throughout the Bible, we read of the birth of churches—*after* disciples are made. Biblical church planting is evangelism that results in new churches. Another way to consider this concept is that it is evangelism that results in new disciples, who then gather to-

gether and self-identify as the local expression of the universal
body of Christ. Churches are supposed to be birthed from disciple
making. (For more introductory information on church planting,
see chapter one in *Discovering Church Planting*.)

THE FOUR NECESSITIES

What is needed to plant a church? Is a capable, charismatic leader
necessary? A polished worship pastor? What about $100,000 in the
bank? A great sound system? A committed core group? A great
website? A public meeting place? A decent trailer to haul around
chairs, dividers, communion cups and other equipment?

I served with one new church that met in a school. Another
church planter I worked with started a church in a movie theater.
One church planter was an excellent expository preacher. Another
worked hard to develop a wonderful children's ministry from the
start. Another was a gifted administrator who established complex
ministry systems. One church planter began with an excellent
worship team. One had a great deal of money for the work. Another had very little.

While these resources are not wrong to have, they are not necessary for a church to be birthed. Many church planters make
these—and other things—primary. But an examination of
Scripture reveals four things that are needed, which I rarely hear
listed as primary.

In Acts 17:1-8, we read of the birth of the church in Thessalonica
during Paul's second missionary journey. While Luke records
some of the big picture elements of the story during the three
weeks or so the team was in the city, Paul later writes two letters
to the church. In the first chapter of his first letter, we get a sense
for what was required for the Thessalonian church to be planted.
Paul writes:

For we know, brothers loved by God, that he has chosen you, because our gospel came to you not only in word, but also in power and in the Holy Spirit and with full conviction. You know what kind of men we proved to be among you for your sake. And you became imitators of us and of the Lord. (1 Thess 1:4-6)

What we find here is that sowers came, sowing the seed in Spirit-prepared soil.[1] Nothing fancy. Nothing flashy. Nothing slick. Nothing complex.

The team evangelized. Some people believed and others did not believe. Those that did believe became imitators of the team in the faith. Although their maturity, zeal and gifts were not the same as the members of the church-planting team, what was necessary for them to be disciples and to make disciples as a local expression of the body of Christ was provided by the Spirit and shown to them through the team in a short period of time. The team was "like a nursing mother taking care of her own children" and "affectionately desirous of" the new believers, sharing with them "not only the gospel of God but also our own selves" (1 Thess 2:7-8). The result was something wonderful. The church in Thessalonica "became an example to all the believers in Macedonia and in Achaia" and the word of the Lord spread from them. Their faith went forth "everywhere" (1 Thess 1:7-8).

Is church planting a difficult ministry? Yes! Absolutely. After reflecting on years of experience in church planting, a friend of mine told me, "You know, J. D., I've found that some of the greatest spiritual highs in my life came while I was involved in church planting." Before I could respond, he quickly added, "But some of my greatest spiritual lows also came about during my church-planting ministry."

Passages abound that show the spiritual opposition and physical persecution that comes with kingdom advancement. Just read the account of the planting of the Thessalonian church and Paul's corresponding letters. The preaching of the gospel and the conversion of the Thessalonians was enough to start a riot! The team was referred to as "men who have turned the world upside down" (Acts 17:6).

However, we are often guilty of making church-planting ministry much more complex than we find it in the Bible. Church planting is about making disciples, baptizing them and teaching them to obey all that Jesus commanded—in covenant community with other kingdom citizens.

Difficult? Yes! Complicated? No. The Father, Son and Holy Spirit did—and continue to do—the complicated and complex part.

SUMMARY

- Biblical church planting is evangelism that results in new churches.

- The four necessities for planting churches are sowers, seed, soil and the Spirit.

- Church planters are to set an imitable model before the new believers.

- Church planting is a difficult ministry but not a complex one.

two

How's Your Ecclesiology?

• • •

Because I am writing to evangelical church planters and pastors in the West who generally hold to a high view of the Bible, Christology (the doctrine of Christ) and soteriology (the doctrine of salvation), the most critical issue in church planting I must address is that of ecclesiology (the doctrine of the Church). How your team defines *church* (local and universal) will affect everything you do in church planting. The definition will affect what your team is trying to plant. It will affect the strategy. It will affect available resources, methods and who can pastor new churches. Ecclesiology is supremely important. It shapes everything.

The Bible refers to the universal Church (I'll use a capital *C* when referring to this) as all those across the ages who have repented of their sin and placed their faith in the Messiah. There are people living today in other parts of the world who we will never meet but who are our brothers and sisters in Christ. We are part of the universal body with them. When Jesus spoke of building his Church (Mt 16:18), he was referring to the universal Church.

However, just as important, the Bible also refers to the local church (I'll use a lowercase *c* when referring to this) as members of his body in a specific location. When Jesus speaks of taking matters of conflict before the church, he was referring to a local assembly

(Mt 18:17). Jesus also refers to local churches in Ephesus, Smyrna, Pergamum, Thyatira, Sardis, Philadelphia and Laodicea (Rev 2–3). Paul writes letters to believers in Colossae, Philippi, Corinth and other locations. The bulk of Paul's New Testament epistles are addressed to specific congregations of saints in these cities: local churches.

To be a believer is to be a member of the universal Church, but there is also an expectation that believers will be participants in a local church. It is impossible to carry out total obedience to Jesus without a commitment to a local expression of his body. Just as the Thessalonians became imitators of the team, we should look to the first century believers as examples to follow in this matter. If we expect new believers to unite together as local churches, our teams also need strong commitments to local churches. It is difficult to tell others to imitate us if we are poor examples.

Over the years I have been asked many questions about church planting. Throughout this book I will share some of the most commonly asked questions, as well as my responses.

Question: What is the local church?

Answer: The local church is the local expression of the universal body of Christ.

Question: When does the church come into existence?

Answer: The church comes into existence when people repent of their sin and place their faith in Jesus, are baptized, and agree to unite together (self-identify) as followers of Jesus in community with one another, as a local expression of his universal body.

Question: But aren't these answers too simplistic? What about pastors? What about worship gatherings? What about deacons? What about evangelism? What about ministry? What about communion? What about small groups? What about Bible study?

What about taking care of orphans and widows? What about engaging culture with a Christian worldview? What about all of those purposes and marks and other characteristics that we have been told must be in place for a church to be a church?

Answer: These are all very important and essential elements of local churches. They are the things new churches ought to grow toward as soon as possible.

PLANT THE CHURCH THAT IS, NOT THE CHURCH TO COME

Hasty expectations hinder the birth and multiplication of churches. On numerous occasions I have heard things like: "Plant your churches, but just make sure they have all of this stuff, and these structures, and these activities, and these twenty-five characteristics, and these forty-one purposes, and this affiliation, and give this amount of money. . . ." Many church planters want to clone or reproduce their home churches—or some other well-established church that is a manifestation of sanctification over a long period of time. They want to plant something trendy. They end up starting instant churches that are very difficult to reproduce or sustain, with a complex organization and structure.

This philosophy is fine when we start churches with long-term kingdom citizens. Those disciples already have years of sanctification behind them. They have a long history of church expectations. We should expect much from these churches since much has been given to their members over time. But this is not the same thing as church planting through disciple making.

Planting churches with longtime believers ought to be the exception to the rule. There is a place for it—indeed, most of my church-planting experience has been with this approach. However, we should permit it as the exception, not the expectation. It is not the regulative paradigm in the New Testament. The weight of the biblical evidence is that churches should be birthed from the harvest fields. Biblical church planting is evangelism that results in new churches, not the shifting of sheep around the kingdom. Beginning with a biblical ecclesiology is important because it keeps us from having unrealistic expectations for churches planted with new disciples from the recent harvest. These churches just started the sanctification process.

- Don't expect them to manifest the same maturity level as a church that is ten, twenty or fifty years old.

- Don't measure them against actions our Father expects them to grow into over time.

- Don't hinder newborn believers by telling them they should be running immediately; they just started crawling.

Church planters are to work with new believers from the beginning. They are not beginning with longtime kingdom citizens who can answer all the Bible trivia questions and can discuss complex doctrines and church history. These people are new believers! In the beginning, the new church is composed of new believers.

From 1978 to 1996, George and Harriett Walker joined Bob and Noby Kennell to serve among the Bisorio people, a remote and unreached tribe in Papua New Guinea. They were introduced to the Bisorio by a neighboring tribe. As the team introduced medicine to the tribe for the first time, the Bisorios' health began to improve dramatically. After the first contact with the tribe, when Bob said he wanted to tell the Bisorio about their creator God, they responded, "Please live with us and tell us about him because we are not happy living the way we are."

The Bisorio did not have a written language, so the team did language learning, alphabet development and eventually Bible translation for them. For three years, the team lived in very close context with the people. George said they could hear their neighbors in the hut next door snoring at night.

One day Bob and George asked the tribal leaders if they could begin telling them "the important story" around the fire at night. During their time with the Bisorio, the team had modeled before the unbelievers what a follower of Jesus was like. Having observed the Christian lifestyle of the team and realizing the importance of the story, the leaders responded to the request by saying that if the story was that important, then everyone in the village needed to hear it. For the next six months Bob and George shared stories from Genesis to the Gospels five days a week.

In 1981 they started doing chronological Bible teaching. George described this evangelistic method as "revolutionary in my mind" and said that it had an "unbelievable impact" on the Bisorio.

Through the use of chronological Bible teaching and interpretive drama, the team shared the message of redemption, and following these six months of teaching, a large number of the tribe repented and placed their faith in Jesus.

Following this great awakening, the new believers were baptized and a church was planted.

Once a group is baptized and self-identify as a church, it is the local church. It is the local expression of the body of Christ, with a great deal to learn and practice. It does not become the local church later, when the people can explain with precision the kenosis passage in Philippians 2, or can execute a liturgy like that found in a cathedral, or when they have complex ministries in place or a budget the size of a small corporation.

Are they a regenerate, baptized group who self-identify as a local expression of the body of Christ? Have they covenanted before the Lord and one another to live out the kingdom ethic (found in the Word) in relation to God, each other and the world—not fully understanding what all that means but willing to do it because Jesus expects it of them?

If so, then you have planted a church that is poised for the multiplication of disciples, leaders and more churches. You have planted the church that *is*.

It does not look cool.

Nothing hip here.

But it is definitely something to write home about!

PLANT THE CHURCH THAT IS, AND HAVE HIGH EXPECTATIONS

Some church planters are so eager to see a church-planting movement occur that they either fail to plant churches at all and just start some groups, or they plant the bare minimum for a local church to exist without any expectations, teaching or leadership development as a part of their church-planting strategy. They reach them and leave them.

Hold this church to high expectations. Your team should teach these disciples the Word and how to study and apply it both privately and in community. The Spirit and the Word will sanctify them. All of those other marks, purposes, manifestations and expectations will come (some more quickly than others) as they are built up in Christ (Col 2:6-7; 1 Pet 2:1-5).

Remember, he is able to keep them from stumbling and to present them blameless before the Father (Jude 24).

Question: What about pastors? You haven't mentioned them yet.

Answer: Pastoral leadership will be addressed in a later chapter. Until then, suffice it to say that while a local church can exist without elders (Acts 14:23; Tit 1:5), it should not exist for very long without them. The church is not defined by its leaders, but leaders are essential to a local church being and functioning as a healthy body.

Question: Your definition doesn't include the Lord's Supper. Can a church exist without partaking in communion?

Answer: Communion is one of the two ordinances (the other being baptism) given by Jesus to his church. It is something the church *does*, not what the church *is*. A church can be birthed without partaking of communion on that day. As soon as possible, however, the church-planting team should show the church what the Bible teaches regarding this ordinance.

Question: Can a church exist without practicing corrective discipline?

Answer: Yes—but again, church discipline is something the church *does*, not what it *is*. It is an action. As soon as possible, the church should be taught about both formative and corrective discipline.

Question: What about preaching? What about worship gatherings? Your definition did not include these.

Answer: Corporate gatherings and the Word rightly preached are both necessary for local churches to be healthy expressions of the universal body of Christ. But these are actions the church does, not who it is.

Question: You keep making a distinction between who the church *is* and what it *does*. Why?

Answer: This distinction is intentional. The church's essence and actions are different. Most people define the church by what it *does*—its functions—and immediately assume that if a new church is not doing these things from the beginning, it is not truly a church.

Closely connected to this is the assumption that our own cultural understanding of a church's functions is normative. The result is that a local church is defined not so much by its actions as by our cultural understanding of those actions. So if a new church does not *immediately* manifest the functions I expect, based on my cultural preferences, then I don't consider that group a church, or I consider it an unhealthy church.

But if a regenerate, baptized group of Jesus' disciples, who self-identify as his called-out ones, purpose to live according to the kingdom ethic in community with one another, then the Spirit who has baptized the church and the ethic found in the Word will lead them to the functions necessary to such a commitment. If they are followers of Jesus, then there will be right actions observed in individuals, families and the church body. Jesus has chosen them to bear fruit (Jn 14:15; 15:16).

Making this distinction enables church-planting teams to recognize that the biblical requirements for a new church are likely to be less than the team's cultural, denominational or traditional preferences and expectations. The distinction also forces teams to grapple with biblical ecclesiology since that is what they have to teach the new churches. Church planters must not only be good missiologists but also good theologians. To be one without the other is to hinder church planting.

Plant the church that *is* and let them function as the church described in the Word. (For more information on ecclesiology and church planting, see chapters two and three in *Discovering Church Planting*.)

SUMMARY

- Our doctrine of the church affects everything we do in church planting.

- A biblical understanding of both the universal Church and the local church is necessary.

- Commitment to Jesus, baptism and self-identification as Christians are essential for a local church to be birthed.

- Planting instant churches with longtime believers should be the exception, not the rule.

- Planting churches from the harvest should be the expectation.

- Plant the church that *is*; maintain high expectations for the church to come.

three

Practices of Team Members

• • •

The history of the United States comprises a rugged individualism, spirit of independence and self-support. The lone ranger is seen as a hero—the one who is able to get the job done on his or her own, answering to no one. Dependence on those outside of ourselves is thought to be a limitation and a challenge to greatness. But the kingdom of God relies on a different value, one that places a great emphasis on partnership and community.

Ministry has always been a team sport. While we do find examples in the Bible of individuals serving the Lord on their own (such as Elijah in 1 Kings 17–19 or Philip in Acts 8), the model of people colaboring takes priority. This is most evident in the disciple-making and church-planting efforts of the apostolic church. In the Gospels we read that Jesus sent out the seventy-two in teams (Lk 10:1), and the first missionaries from Antioch were the team of Paul and Barnabas (Acts 13:2-3). In God's economy, the missionary team is vital to the propagation of the gospel and the multiplication of disciples, leaders and churches.

Resources abound on the topics of team formation and development, team leadership, and the strengths and limitations of teams. In this chapter, however, I want to turn your attention to eight essential characteristics of church-planting team members.

Teams need different gifts, talents and skills. Having a team consisting of church planters who share the same attributes will mean that the team will be very strong in a few areas but limited in others. An examination of Paul's writings makes it clear that the body of Christ comprises different gifts (1 Cor 12) and different offices (Eph 4:11-12). While a church-planting team is not the same as the church, they are part of the church. Diversity is a good thing.

However, the following eight practices are universals. Healthy manifestations of these practices should be present for each team member, regardless of their personal gifts.

I refer to these as the Barnabas Factors because they are significant characteristics from the life of Barnabas that can be applied to contemporary church-planting teams. (For more information on church-planting teams, see chapter fifteen in *Discovering Church Planting* as well as my book *The Barnabas Factors: Eight Essential Practices of Church Planting Team Members.*[1])

We often think of Barnabas as just an encourager and overlook his contributions to kingdom expansion. But the Scriptures are clear that he was significantly involved in first century church-planting work. If there had been no Barnabas to embrace and vouch for Paul in Jerusalem and Antioch, it is unlikely that Paul would have become the church planter we know him to be (Acts 9:26-28; 11:25).

Barnabas was recognized as a servant, teacher, leader and apostle (Acts 14:14). He was described as "our beloved Barnabas" (Acts 15:25), a son of encouragement (Acts 4:36), and "a good man, full of the Holy Spirit and of faith" (Acts 11:24). We first read of him as a member of the Jerusalem church. He made great sacrifices for this congregation and for the spread of the gospel. Yet, even with his outstanding reputation, he was not immune to conflict and the sin of hypocrisy.

I once knew of a church planter who was willing to have anyone on his team as long as they were breathing air and loved Jesus. This is a plan for disaster! While the "air/love test" may sound like a romantic idea, it should not be a standard for team membership.

Personal histories should be considered. Qualities desired in a team should be present in the individuals' lives long before they enter the field. This is important not only for the team's health, but also because the qualities and characteristics of the team will be passed on to the new churches. Although God is in the sanctification business, our past behaviors (as believers) are some of the best predictors of how we will act in the future. Team members may have all the desired knowledge and skills, but if they lack these eight biblical practices, they will not be a wise inclusion on a church-planting team.

What are the Barnabas Factors? A team member who demonstrates Barnabas's characteristics is someone who:

Walks with the Lord. It was out of his relationship with the Lord that Barnabas was able to serve wisely and well. It is unlikely that the Spirit would have called him if he was out of fellowship with God (Acts 13:2). If he regularly grieved the Spirit, it's hard to believe that he and Paul could have given an account of the work of the Spirit to the Jerusalem Council (Acts 15). Barnabas called others to remain true to the Lord with a resolute heart (Acts 11:23). His walk with God made him lovable (Acts 15:25), reliable (Acts 11:30), bold (Acts 13:46) and resilient (Acts 13:50-51).

The desire to accomplish great things for the Lord should never interfere with a team's walk with the Lord. To obey him is better than sacrifice (1 Sam 15:22). Walking faithfully with the Lord enables the team to know how to live in relation to God, other team members and those outside of the kingdom. I once heard a church planter say, "Church planting is walking with God and hanging out with people." While this is a little simplistic, the point is well made. It begins with an intimate fellowship with the Father, Son and Spirit.

Maintains an outstanding character. Barnabas is described as a good man (Acts 11:24). In all likelihood this description came from his outstanding character that revealed itself by a gentle spirit, good actions and good speech. He is also described as being full of the Holy Spirit and faith (Acts 11:24). He was able to trust God for provision and for future ministry possibilities.

The character of team members is critical for unity and effectiveness. It is what they will model before others. Team members should be full of the Holy Spirit (Eph 5:18), constantly yielding themselves to the Lord. Goodness and faith should also describe them. A church planter once shared with me, "Great leadership is built on trust. Without character, trust can never be achieved. If you aren't a person of integrity, the effort will implode quickly."

Serves the local church. The first mention of Barnabas in the Bible describes him selling a piece of property and giving the money to the Jerusalem church (Acts 4:32-37). He is described in this passage as the "son of encouragement." The leaders of the church trusted him enough that they sent him to Antioch to spend a year there encouraging and teaching the new believers (Acts 11:22). He was a man who encouraged, sacrificed for and submitted to the church.

How a team serves is a reflection of their feelings toward themselves as well as others. Teams should consist of members who love the church and sacrifice for her. Teams reproduce what they know and what they have experienced. If the team longs to see new believers become fruit-bearing disciples in a local church, then the team members must manifest this commitment themselves.

Remains faithful to the call. We are not told when Barnabas was converted. It is possible that it occurred on the day of Pentecost (Acts 2). He is simply introduced as a faithful member of the Jerusalem church (Acts 4). It was out of this ministry in Antioch that the Spirit called him to church planting (Acts 13:1-3). This calling came out of Barnabas's faithfulness to the Lord, the team and the Great Commission, especially during times of persecution.

Great challenges of spiritual warfare and persecution are likely to come to any church-planting team. Members should be faithful to God's calling on their lives. Days will come when it will be the only thing that keeps them on the field.

Of course, there are other issues that may arise that could distract church planters from their calling. At the time of this writing, our church is planning to commission Jeff and Julie to be sent out as church planters. Twenty-four hours after they agreed that the Lord was leading them in this ministry direction, another church contacted Jeff to let him know that they were seriously considering him to be their next pastor, and that they would provide a substantial financial package. Though Jeff and Julie considered it an honor that this church contacted them and gave serious thought to the opportunity, they declined. "God has called us to this church-planting ministry," Jeff shared. "That is all we need."

Shares the gospel regularly. Barnabas knew that church planting began with evangelism. In all likelihood he agreed with Paul that church planters must become all things to all people in order to save some (1 Cor 9:22). His work as an evangelist was done with intentionality (Acts 13:50-51; 14:1-6). He was bold (Acts 13:46). He responded to persecution with a tenacity to continue to share the gospel (Acts 14:6-7). He preferred to work among receptive people and was willing to shake the dust off his feet and move on when necessary (Acts 13:51). And although he was significantly engaged in evangelism, he was also concerned with the spiritual maturity of those who came to faith. It was not enough to make disciples without teaching them in the context of local churches with their leaders (Acts 14:21-23).

Intentional, regular evangelism is one nonnegotiable practice of church-planting teams. If teams are not significantly engaged in such work, disciples will not be made and churches will not be planted. This is the first step on the "pathway to planting" (see chap. 4). As with the other Barnabas Factors, team members should have a history of regular evangelism.

For several years, James Harvey served as a church planter in Nashville, Tennessee, among the largest concentration of Kurdish Muslims in the United States. While he did a great deal of ministry to meet the needs of the people, he took a long time to introduce the gospel message. Often so much time had gone by in the relationship that it was awkward to finally share the gospel. In my conversation with James, he confessed, "I had to repent of my lack of evangelism." James decided to change his method and started identifying himself as a Christ-follower and sharing the gospel as early as possible in his encounters with people. Though he has not seen any Kurds come to faith yet, he has witnessed the salvation of other unreached people in his community, and he is beginning home Bible studies and working to plant churches among them, while still praying for and sharing with the Kurds.

Raises up leaders. Barnabas spent time with other leaders. His reputation was known among the elders and apostles in the Jerusalem church. He also practiced wisdom-guided risk taking when it came to developing leaders. We often forget that it was Barnabas who vouched for Paul when the other leaders in Jerusalem feared him. Barnabas was willing to take a chance with Paul, knowing of the truth of Paul's conversion (Acts 9:27). It was because of Barnabas's ability to see the potential in Paul that others embraced this persecutor-turned-preacher (Acts 9:28). Barnabas also saw the possibility in John Mark for a leader. On the second missionary journey, Paul refused to take John Mark on the team since John Mark had deserted them on the previous journey (Acts 13:13). But Barnabas was willing to give him a second chance (Acts 15:38-39).

The first step on the "pathway to planting" is sharing the gospel, and the last step is appointing pastors. Teams should consist of members who refuse to do all the work. Rather, they recognize their calling to an equipping ministry, laboring for the empowering and releasing of others to do the work. Raising up leaders is another nonnegotiable practice. It involves teaching others right doctrine *and* right practice. Some excellent resources to assist with leadership development include Neil Cole and Robert Logan, *Raising Leaders for the Harvest*; Robert Coleman, *The Master Plan of Evangelism*; and Steve Smith with Ying Kai, *T4T: A Discipleship Re-Revolution*.[2]

Encourages with speech and actions. In the Bible, names were sometimes given based on a person's characteristics. Barnabas's birth name was Joseph. Sometime after Pentecost, the apostles gave him the name Barnabas, meaning "son of encouragement" or "son of consolation" (Acts 4:36). As a result of his relationship with the Great Encourager, Barnabas was a man whose words and actions were above reproach. His speech was trustworthy, true and consistent. He convinced the church in Jerusalem that Paul was a genuine believer (Acts 9:27). He was a teacher of God's Word (Acts 11:26). Even when Paul was not willing to bring John Mark on the second journey, Barnabas showed his consistency: having vouched for Paul in Jerusalem, he now stood with John Mark against Paul. Barnabas's actions were substantial, sacrificial and helpful, and they set an example for others to follow. Barnabas strengthened the faith of many by sacrificing his money and time.

Commenting on the significance of encouragement in church-planting teams, one church planter shared with me: "Encouragement is key. In church planting, you have to look for things to be encouraged about and to encourage each other about. Encouragement is a cornerstone of church planting."

I asked another church planter about how he encouraged his team. He said it did not come easy, but that encouragement was a must. He wrote,

> I always try to communicate how valuable each one of them is to me personally and to the ministry. . . . I would say this is not my greatest strength, so I need to be very intentional to accomplish this. . . . Help them feel like they are part of *your* team, not just *the* team. Let them feel valued by you.

Church-planting teams experience many difficult days in the field. Encouragement is greatly needed. Often the only people who encourage the team are the team members themselves.

Responds appropriately to conflict. Where two or three people are gathered in the name of Jesus, there will be conflict. This should not be a surprise. Mistakes and misunderstandings will occur. Church-planting teams are composed of forgiven people, but forgiven people are still sinners. And even when sin is not present, conflict still happens.

Barnabas and Paul had such a sharp disagreement over whether or not to bring John Mark with them on their missionary journey that they went their separate ways. Paul took Silas and traveled to Syria and Cilicia, strengthening the churches. Barnabas took John Mark and traveled to Cyprus (Acts 15:36-41). Paul also experienced great disappointment and conflict as a result of Barnabas's hypocrisy (Gal 2:13). From Paul's reference to Barnabas in his letter to the Corinthians, we may conclude that these disagreements did not sever the relationship between Paul and Barnabas (1 Cor 9:6). The relationship between Paul and John Mark also continued (Col 4:10), with Paul even saying that John Mark was "useful" to him (2 Tim 4:11).

When times of conflict arise, teams must respond appropriately. Everything must be done out of love for the sake of the kingdom and the witness of the team. A spirit of humility, servanthood and seeking the best for the other team members must be present. No one enjoys conflict, but it will occur. Not all conflict is bad, but sometimes teams must separate due to the matter at hand.

SUMMARY

The Barnabas Factors remind us that there is much more to being a good church-planting team member than knowing the answers to theological or missiological questions. Healthy spiritual practices in the individuals' lives are critical for healthy teams.

Knowing if the Barnabas Factors are present in other people's lives when you consider inviting them to join your team—or accept an invitation from them to join their team—is best discerned in community. Yes, it is a good idea to talk with other people who have ministered with these brothers and sisters. But there is no substitute for personal interaction with others in the context of a local church. This is one reason why church-planting teams should be developed within local churches.

When considering partnering on a team with someone, take a moment to evaluate them in light of the Barnabas Factors. Yes, this will be a subjective exercise, but as the team leader you have a right to be subjective. You know who and what you are looking for regarding the task to come. Take time to reread the above descriptions of the Barnabas Factors, and for each factor, evaluate the person on the following scale:

Low	Medium	High

| 1 | 2 | 3 | 4 | 5 | 6 | 7 | 8 | 9 | 10 |

I suggest that as you seek the Lord's will regarding potential members of your team, you total up the numbers and consider the following guide:

- Low total (8-24): Do not select this person for the team.

- Medium total (32-56): Consider inviting this individual to the team with strong reservations and conditions for development. Identify where this person scored low on the Barnabas Factors and provide guidance for growth.

- High total (64-80): A high total still doesn't necessarily guarantee effectiveness. It does suggest that this person strongly manifests the Barnabas Factors necessary for healthy team members. Consider inviting this individual to the team.

four

Pathway to Planting

• • •

An examination of the apostle Paul's first missionary journey (and the corresponding epistles) provides a glimpse of the steps followed by his first century church-planting teams. Though the Bible was not written with the primary purpose of teaching future generations how to plant churches, there is much we can learn by simply reading the text. Our context is different than Paul's, but Roland Allen was correct when he wrote, "Either we must drag down St. Paul from his pedestal as the great missionary, or else we must acknowledge that there is in his work that quality of universality."[1] I hear many church planters refer to Paul as the "greatest church planter," yet few are willing to learn from him. They want his theology and results but not his principles. Let's hope this changes. While we should not attempt to replicate first-century culture, we should prayerfully and wisely discern the biblical principles demonstrated by Paul and his missionary teams and imitate them as we contextualize our efforts in today's world, where billions of people are without Christ.

Acts 13–14 lay out these early missionaries' procedure for church planting. Paul and Barnabas are on their first missionary journey. After being sent from the church in Antioch (Acts 13:1-3), they travel through Salamis, Pisidia-Antioch, Iconium, Lystra and Derbe. They enter these cities and begin sharing the gospel (Acts 13:5, 16; 14:1, 9).

Two results follow: some people repent and believe in Jesus, and others do not. Those who do not often persecute the team or even run them out of town (Acts 13:50; 14:5, 19). The team then travels to the next city, and the cycle repeats itself.

Near the end of the first missionary journey, however, Luke makes a fascinating summary statement. Instead of moving on to new cities to continue the cycle, the team backtracks to the cities in which they had just planted churches.

> They returned to Lystra and to Iconium and to Antioch, strengthening the souls of the disciples, encouraging them to continue in the faith, and saying that through many tribulations we must enter the kingdom of God. And when they had appointed elders for them in every church, with prayer and fasting they committed them to the Lord in whom they had believed. (Acts 14:21-23)

A few questions can help us understand what happened on the first missionary journey related to a pathway to planting:

- Where did the elders (that is, pastors) for the churches come from?
- Where did the churches in the cities come from?
- Where did the disciples in the cities come from?

WHERE DID THE ELDERS COME FROM?

The pastors for these churches came from the new disciples that made up the newly planted churches. While this answer may come as a surprise to those of us living in places where the church has existed for centuries, it's true. Paul and Barnabas had a small team,

so all of the elders could not have come from their team. There is
no record of the team contacting the churches in Antioch or Jerusalem asking, "Could you please send us some pastors for these new
churches?" There were no seminaries to recruit from. They couldn't
post a "help wanted" ad in a denominational newspaper.

Church leaders were imperative for the health and mission of
the local churches. While the churches existed before the pastors
were appointed, the team knew that church leadership had to be
put in place as soon as possible. So they saw that leaders were appointed, even before the first missionary journey ended.

Did these pastors preach thirty-minute monological sermons
every week? I doubt it. Were they capable of sitting on committees
and overseeing the youth group and the praise and worship team?
Unlikely.

Assuming that Paul followed the same model on his other
missionary journeys, additional biblical texts help illustrate what
may have happened on that first journey. For example, we read
in Acts 19 and 20 that Paul stayed in Ephesus for three years
(Acts 20:31)—and in all likelihood the elders were in place during
that time (Acts 20:17)—before he left the city for Macedonia
(Acts 20:1). He later sent Timothy to Ephesus to work with the
elders and the church in the city. We have the honor of reading
Paul's counsel and exhortation to Timothy in the two letters that
bear his name.

We find further evidence of the importance of pastors in newly
planted churches in Paul's epistle to Titus, where Paul reminds
him of his reason for being in Crete. Paul writes, "This is why I
left you in Crete, so that you might put what remained into order,
and appoint elders in every town as I directed you" (Titus 1:5).
Crete was an island with towns dotting the landscape. If we allow
Scripture to interpret Scripture, then we remember from the first

missionary journey (Acts 13–14) that church planting did not begin with training pastors who would then find churches to serve—or even plant churches to serve. Instead, the churches came first and then the pastors. Given this part of the pathway to planting, we can assume that churches were in existence across Crete but were without elders. Paul had directed Titus to appoint elders before he sent the letter and reminds him of this in his correspondence.

Question: Paul writes to Timothy that an elder "must not be a recent convert, or he may become puffed up with conceit and fall into the condemnation of the devil" (1 Tim 3:6). How are we to reconcile Paul's own missionary methods with what he writes to Timothy here? Is Paul contradicting himself by appointing new converts as elders and then telling Timothy to avoid doing just that?

Answer: Some writers have responded to this concern by arguing that because Paul only writes this mandate to Timothy in Ephesus, and not to Titus in Crete, the mandate must have only been applicable to the church in Ephesus.

While all Scripture was written in specific cultural contexts and to people in different situations, this is not a good enough reason to claim that the "recent convert" mandate only applied to Ephesus. Given the context of 1 Timothy 3 (where Paul is giving a list of prerequisites for church leadership), it seems that Paul is establishing a more universal principle.

Others argue that Paul only mentions this rule to Timothy because elders were already in place in Ephesus but not in Crete. Because elders were already established in Ephesus, a new convert who was quickly appointed as an elder could easily become "puffed up with conceit" (1 Tim 3:6) when placed in such an important role alongside other, more mature elders.

This argument does have more merit than the first, taking into consideration both the historical context of the Ephesian church and the text of 1 Timothy 3. But it still seems that there is something more universal about 1 Timothy 3 (and Titus 1). If this second argument is right, and Paul is only addressing Ephesus specifically here, then much of his letters—and the rest of the Bible—becomes applicable only to the people, locations and times in which they were written.

We know that Paul appointed elders during his first missionary journey, even though these elders could not have been Christians for very long. He also later appointed elders in Ephesus, even though he spent only three years working there. So where does this leave us in regard to Paul's words to Timothy? It appears that either:

- Paul contradicted himself;

- Paul was trying to correct his previous mistakes with new instructions in 1 Timothy 3; or

- we are reading our cultural expectations into the words "recent convert" and assuming more than was necessary in the first century.

I do not believe Paul contradicted himself or that he was attempting to correct himself. I do think we have misunderstood this text in light of our cultural preferences. Let me try to explain.

In the brief amount of time Paul was with the Ephesian elders, he taught them the whole counsel of God (Acts 20:26-27). Elders were overseeing the Ephesian church within three years of its birth and overseeing the new churches of the first missionary journey (which only lasted two years). Similarly, the twelve apostles were in leadership roles after Jesus spent just three years with them. All this suggests that it is biblically permissible for such people—that is, "uneducated, common men" (Acts 4:13)—to be in leadership roles only a short while after their conversions.

"Recent" seems to have to do with maturity as well as a period of time. This "length of time" can be an expectation we arbitrarily determine, but we are two thousand years removed from the biblical context and are members of mature churches that have been around for a long time.

"Recent" obviously does have a time element. The only way to know if a person manifested the qualifications of an elder found in 1 Timothy 3 and Titus 1 was for the church to spend time in community with that person. How can we know whether a potential leader is hospitable (1 Tim 3:3), manages their household well (1 Tim 3:4), has a good reputation with outsiders (1 Tim 3:7), is not arrogant (Titus 1:7) but is self-controlled (Titus 1:8), without spending some time with them and their family? It is difficult to know such information from a person's résumé, even if you call their references.

The Spirit does not always work on the same schedule in every situation. Sometimes the sanctification process is faster, other times it is slower. The time between the conversion of the new believers and the appointment of the first pastors will differ from context to context. I have heard some church planters in India and China speak of such appointments happening within a few months of those leaders coming to faith.

Brad Buser's situation was different. Brad and his family served among the Iteri people of Papua New Guinea from 1979 till 1999. The Iteri were a remote, impoverished, illiterate and nomadic people. "When we arrived," Brad said, "we had to hack out an airstrip to get supplies in and out of the area." By 1986, after seven months of Bible storying, twenty-two people came to faith and were baptized—the first believers among this people. But, although a church was planted, the first six elders were not appointed until 1995.

If we remember that Christian community was necessary to determine whether a person manifested the qualifications for an elder, it should not come as a surprise that the pastors of the churches Paul planted came from the churches. The pastors were of the people and from the people. The people all came into the kingdom at approximately the same time. The churches were very simple in structure and organization. The members of these churches (including the pastors) were familiar with the apostle's teaching. They had an intimate connection with Paul and his companions. They were to hold one another accountable (1 Cor 5; Phil 4:2-3) to the gospel entrusted to them. Pastors were not equipped or expected to oversee the complex cultural structures and organizations that have since developed across the centuries in many church traditions.

Paul wrote to Timothy that pastors were to be "able to teach" (1 Tim 3:2). A pastor was to "hold firm to the trustworthy word as taught, so that he may be able to give instruction in sound doctrine and also to rebuke those who contradict it" (Tit 1:9). When we read these words today, we often filter them through our contemporary church traditions. We assume that these passages mean that a pastor must have a Bible college or seminary degree, be able to stand before a crowd uninterrupted and teach a Bible passage for at least thirty minutes, be able to debate the scholarly atheists of our day, know Greek and Hebrew, understand the teachings of Arminianism and Calvinism, explain the major church councils, creeds and heresies, and teach correctly about pre-, post- and amillennialism.

Now, is there anything wrong with pastors being able to do these things? Of course not! Such abilities and knowledge are good. However, they are not requirements for a pastor. Pastors are like other Christians: they are being sanctified and are developing their gifts, skills and knowledge.

I once had lunch with a renowned theologian and a renowned missionary. Let's call them Augustine and Carey. Augustine had his formative training in western seminaries. His ministry experience included pastoring a church that had a long heritage and was home to many seminary students. Carey had served in remote areas of the Muslim world. As we enjoyed our lunch, Carey made a passing comment that new pastors need to be grounded in the Word of God but did not need to know all the theories of the atonement when they began overseeing the churches.

Augustine interrupted and asked for clarification. Carey explained that we need to teach the Bible and not complicate matters for new pastors on secondary issues. For the next several minutes, Augustine pointed out Carey's error and began to wax eloquently on the need to understand such theories and how they are practical to pastoral ministry. Carey shot back with a rebuttal, noting Augustine's lack of cultural intelligence. It was awkward.

Who was right? They both were right, to a degree. The problem was that they were communicating with two completely different contexts in mind. Though they were using the same terms, they were operating on different wavelengths. Augustine, who trained seminary students to pastor churches with long histories, was unable to see the simpler nature of the church in a pioneer context and that Majority World, Muslim-background believers could be effective pastors even if they never went to college or seminary—or even if they couldn't read. He was looking at the conversation through the lens of a centuries-old definition of pastoral ministry. Could the pastors with whom Carey worked pastor Augustine's church? No. The cultural expectations for pastoral ministry in that setting were impossible for them to achieve.

Carey, however, saw that this definition of pastoral ministry would hinder the growth and development of the new pastors in the Muslim world. He knew they could barely find Lamentations in the Bible, let alone explain the differences between the recapitulation and ransom theories of atonement. But he was unable to see a future situation in which these pastors (and churches) might need such training.

Too many of our church planting conversations today are on different wavelengths—one for a mature church context, one for a new church context. The result is usually that the mature church perspective dominates, resulting in church-planting activities that are complex, resistant to movement and expensive. This matter is even more complicated in the West where the church has a long heritage in place. It is extremely difficult for many Westerners today to even consider the apostolic nature of church planting in such contexts. Traditional understandings usually win the discussions.

I know more about the Bible now than I did when I started pastoring twenty years ago. If you had asked me during my first pastorate to explain the moral-example theory, I would have pleaded ignorance. If my abilities and sanctification *today* were the standard to which I was held twenty years ago, I would not have been serving as a pastor until very recently—and those abilities and sanctification came largely through the experience of pastoring for twenty years. Unnecessary and arbitrary cultural expectations are often placed on leaders, which can hinder the health of churches and the multiplication of the gospel.

Remember, in the New Testament these pastors were not overseeing churches with long histories. Everyone was fairly new in the kingdom. The elders were shepherding people who were at a fairly similar maturity level—one that was probably close to their own.

Question: Are you saying that since Paul was in Ephesus for three years, Corinth for eighteen months (Acts 18:11) and Thessalonica for as little as three weeks (Acts 17:2), all church planters should be governed by these timeframes?

Answer: No. I do not believe that we can put a timetable on the work of the Holy Spirit to birth churches and appoint elders (Acts 20:28). I make this point because the Bible records this to be the case in these areas. I believe that some church-planting activities can be both healthy and more rapid than many of us think possible. While this is not always the case, we know that the Lord has specifically shown it to be a possibility.

WHERE DID THE CHURCHES IN THE CITIES COME FROM?

The churches were started by gathering the new believers who came to faith through Paul and Barnabas's ministry on the first missionary journey. These new believers were already residents of these communities. They understood the context and culture because it was their context and culture.

No one contacted the church in Jerusalem to ask for one hundred members to be sent with a pastor to Iconium. The church in Antioch did not hive off thirty members to move to Lystra and function as a local church to reach the city with Paul and Barnabas as pastors.

WHERE DID THE DISCIPLES IN THE CITIES COME FROM?

The disciples came from the harvest fields of ministry. Prior to the arrival of the missionary team, these men and women had been separated from God. They may have previously worshipped Zeus and Hermes (Acts 14:11-13) or been connected to a synagogue (Acts 13:5). They had not repented of their sin and placed faith in Jesus. People are not born as disciples of Jesus. While someone's journey of faith is usually a process, there is a moment in time when they are regenerated by the Holy Spirit. One moment they are in the kingdom of darkness, and the next moment they are in the kingdom of light.

A disciple is a follower: someone who believes in Jesus as Lord of all. Disciple making begins with evangelism: calling people to repentance and faith in Jesus. Luke tells us that Paul and Barnabas "preached the gospel to that city and . . . made many disciples" (Acts 14:21).

Here is what we read about the team's actions whenever they entered a city:

- "When they arrived at Salamis, they proclaimed the word of God" (Acts 13:5).

- "So Paul stood up, and motioning with his hand said"(Acts 13:16).

- "Paul and Barnabas, who, as they spoke with them, urged them to continue in the grace of God"(Acts 13:43).

- "Paul and Barnabas spoke out boldly, saying"(Acts 13:46).

- "Now at Iconium they entered together into the Jewish synagogue and spoke in such a way that a great number of both Jews and Greeks believed" (Acts 14:1).

- "So they remained for a long time, speaking boldly for the Lord" (Acts 14:3).

- "They learned of it and fled to Lystra and Derbe, cities of Lycaonia, and to the surrounding country, and there they continue to preach the gospel"(Acts 14:6-7).

An examination of the pathway followed on the first missionary journey reveals at least four steps along the church planting pathway. The following diagram shows the order of this approach:

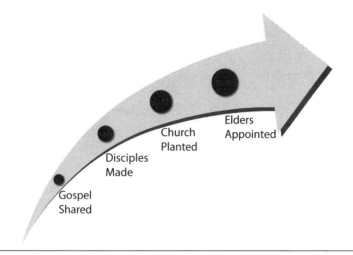

Figure 1. The pathway to planting

SUMMARY

Now that we have answered three important questions about the first missionary journey, let's put them together to see the biblical pathway for church planting.

- First, the team enters the community and evangelizes.
- Second, some people believe and some people do not believe.
- Third, the new believers are called disciples and are gathered together as a new church, the "called-out ones."
- Fourth, the team works with the church to identify and appoint pastors to oversee the church.
- Finally, the team repeats the process elsewhere but returns to visit or maintains communication with the churches and leaders for ongoing teaching, accountability, equipping and partnership in the mission.

The rest of this book is an attempt to offer a practical approach to church planting with this biblical pathway as our guide.

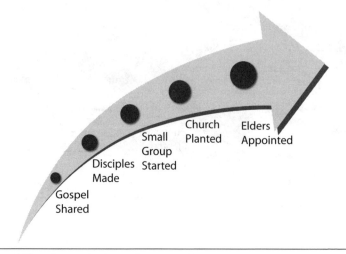

Figure 2. The pathway to planting: small group started

One final addendum. I train church-planting teams to insert another brief step in the pathway to planting process. The new disciples need to know what a local church is before they can self-identify as one. As noted in figure 2, gathering the disciples into a small group allows the team to teach and model in community what it means to be a disciple and to make disciples. Many church-planting teams also have a high regard for small groups. Thus this additional, yet transitional, step in the process is helpful to contemporary teams.

five

Stages of Planting

●●●

When I travel by car to new places, I use my phone's GPS. I usually do not look at paper maps. I just punch in the address and drive. However, I remember that when I was a child and my family traveled on vacation, my mom would get out a road map and study it in detail. She would have the big picture of the trip in mind even before we departed.

The process of church planting can be structured into six broad stages.[1] This categorization will help in the development of the church-planting strategy and clarify where the team is in the church-planting process. In addition to the biblical understanding of the pathway to planting, it is helpful for us to have these six stages in mind as we begin.

THE SIX STAGES OF CHURCH PLANTING

Each stage comes with a primary question that the team must answer. The six stages with their respective questions are:

1. Pre-entry stage: What do we need to do before arriving on the field and how will we do it?

2. Entry stage: How do we enter the field?

3. Gospel stage: How do we connect with people and share the gospel?

4. Discipleship stage: What is necessary for short-term and long-term discipleship?

5. Church formation stage: How will we lead the new believers to self-identify as a church and organize themselves for mission?

6. Leadership stage: How will we model and teach leadership and work with the new believers to appoint pastors?

The six stages are not mutually exclusive. For example, the team will be heavily involved in evangelism in the early days. But as people come to faith the team will be less involved in evangelism and more involved in discipleship and church formation. The team will need to continue to share the gospel, both for their own sanctification as well as to model evangelism before the new believers they are teaching, but the new believers should take on more and more of this Great Commission responsibility. It is only for the ease of understanding that I am describing these stages as a linear process. Though each stage must happen before the subsequent stage, there is no hard and fast transition from one stage to the next.

Like the pathway to planting, the six stages remind us that church planting is about a process. The team should not plan to remain in any one of these stages indefinitely but to move through them with stage-specific strategies and methods. (I will share more about methods later.)

What generally occurs during each stage?

Pre-entry. This initial stage involves everything that the team does prior to arriving on the field. This also applies to domestic church-planting teams who are not preparing for crosscultural ministry. The team asks: What do we need to do before arriving on the field and how do we need to do it? This stage includes developing as a team, studying the culture and context through published resources and conversations with others and language learning (if necessary). The team begins developing their overall strategy during this stage, but they will continue to make adjustments to it throughout the entire church-planting process. The team should make vision trips to the field, find places to live that will facilitate their ministry and secure employment in the community (if necessary). This stage also involves any equipping and assessment that needs to occur with the team before moving to the field.

Entry. The second stage includes everything that the team does as they arrive on the field. The main question the team is asking here is: How do we enter the field as outsiders? The entry stage includes connecting with neighbors, learning where to shop, knowing the local hangouts and gaining more understanding about the cultural context. Although entry issues are the primary matters addressed at this stage, the team should begin sharing the gospel and developing an intentional evangelistic lifestyle as best they can.

The team should consider what passions, talents, skills and interests they have when looking for ways to engage those around them. One Sunday morning, a lady from our church stopped me as I was walking into our worship gathering. She was very excited and wanted to share something with me. She told me that she and another member of our church had been frequenting a nail salon in the city. This particular business was owned by a Vietnamese man, and most of his employees had recently arrived from Vietnam. Each time these ladies would get their nails done, they noticed the shrine to Buddha in the salon and were reminded to pray for the employees and the owner. One day, however, they decided to use their own resources to share the gospel and help improve the business. They approached the owner and asked him if they could teach the ladies English. Knowing that most of the employees spoke broken English, they believed this would help the women and the business. The owner was excited. In fact, he was so excited that he wanted to pay them. Of course, they refused any pay. He opened his store up for the English classes.

Gospel. This stage includes everything the team does related to sharing the gospel through word and actions. (For more information on evangelism and church planting, see chapter six in *Discovering Church Planting.*) The team asks: How do we connect with people and call them to repentance and faith in Jesus alone? The team should be quick to share the gospel with others, even if they are in the initial stages of learning the language of the people. The Spirit is able to work though written resources, electronic material, broken grammar and translators.

The team should be intentional about praying for the work of the Spirit as they go. (For more information on prayer and church planting, see chapter five in *Discovering Church Planting.*) The message should be widely disseminated among the community to as many people as possible. During this stage, the team should share the gospel

- as prayerfully as possible;

- as soon as possible; and

- as widely as possible.

Earlier I shared about James Harvey in Nashville, Tennessee. I recently asked him about his methods during this stage. He shared that he now uses a simple threefold approach when he encounters unreached people groups: (1) He lets people know that he is a follower of Jesus as quickly as possible, (2) he asks them if he could pray for God's blessing for them, and (3) he asks them if they would be interested in studying the Bible in their homes.

Not only has James recognized the significance of sowing the gospel broadly and looking for the most receptive people, but he is also aware of the importance of context and culture when it comes to the gospel stage. "We use this approach to quickly get to the gospel," James said. "This method works here but probably would not work well in a different cultural context."

James provides pastoral leadership to a network of ten churches in Nashville. Each church has set a goal this year: to reproduce themselves in another person's home. Following the example of Luke 10, their strategy is to find "houses of peace" (Lk 10:5-6)—that is, houses belonging to unbelievers who are open to having Bible studies in their home with other unbelievers of their acquaintance.

Church members are told to make sure the Holy Spirit is leading their strategy and to look for spiritually hungry people. During one church meeting, two men felt the Spirit leading them to go immediately across the street to a Somalian-owned coffee shop. They shared this with the church, asked for prayer and walked over to the business. They struck up a conversation with the owner, told him they were followers of Jesus and asked if he would be interested in studying the Bible. For the next twenty minutes, the owner refused to serve his customers so that he could talk with these two men! They began a Bible study in that shop.

Using this Spirit-led approach, being intentional about sharing the gospel and praying with unbelievers for Jesus' blessing on them, members of James's team have also started a Bible study in the home of two Iraqi Muslims and in the home of a Mexican family.

Discipleship. The Great Commission involves more than reaching people with the gospel. It also involves "teaching them to observe" all that Jesus commanded (Mt 28:20). Evangelism is just the tip of the Great Commission iceberg. After people become followers of Jesus, their journey as disciples in community with other disciples continues until glorification. The missionary team must equip and empower these disciples to believe and follow the kingdom ethic as a kingdom community (that is, a local church). The primary question being asked by the team at this stage is: What do these people need for immediate short-term discipleship and for long-term discipleship?

The majority of the team's labors are located in this stage and the next (the church stage), which are tightly connected. Conducting baptisms and teaching spiritual disciplines are primary activities during this time. (For more information on discipleship and church planting, see chapter seven in *Discovering Church Planting*.)

Church. This stage involves leading the new believers to self-identify and covenant together as a local church. Care is taken to teach them biblical ecclesiology. Nathan and Kari Shank write that it is important for the new believers to ask questions such as: (1) Who is the church? (2) When do we meet? (3) Where do we meet? (4) Why do we meet? (5) What do we do?[2] This stage also includes leading the church to appoint elders, mentoring those elders and partnering with the new church to plant other churches.

Leadership. Though we may think that leadership development begins after the appointment of elders, this is not the case. Leadership development begins at least simultaneously with the gospel stage and continues through the discipleship and church stages.

Even when the team is first sharing the gospel with unbelievers, they are modeling what it means to be a leader in the kingdom. So while there are certainly more specific lessons and skills to be addressed after elders are appointed, the team is subtly doing leadership development very early in their work.

In his book *Passing the Baton*, Tom Steffen includes the component of *phase-out* to the church-planting process.[3] Phasing-out involves the team making planned role changes throughout the stages. The team should work to empower the new church to stand on its own through the Word, the Spirit and the church's leaders.

I find it helpful to visualize phase-out as a thread that runs throughout each of the stages.

Phase-Out				
Pre-Entry	Entry	Gospel Leadership Development	Discipleship Leadership Development	Church Leadership Development

Figure 3. Church-planting stages with the phase-out thread

The phase-out thread is based on the notion that *the team begins with its end in mind.* The team intentionally plans to remove itself physically from the new church, even before they arrive on the field. In light of such thinking, the team allows their end desire (that is, a local church engaged in mission with its own leaders) to influence everything they do from the pre-entry stage to the church formation/leadership development stage. If phase-out shapes their thinking, then the team will be careful to develop their strategy with methods that are simple, highly reproducible and imitable so that the gospel may ring out from the new church (1 Thess 1:6-8).

The metaphor of a scaffold has been used throughout history to help missionary teams think about empowering and releasing disciples for ministry. The scaffold on a construction site serves as a temporary fixture—not a permanent structure—until the work is finished. In a similar fashion, the church-planting team recognizes the apostolic nature of their labors and strives to plant a church, lead that church to select pastors and then equip those pastors to lead the church. Once the church is planted and its leaders are in place, the team remains in contact (through visits, communication and partnerships) but moves on to preach the gospel to those who have yet to hear it (Rom 15:14, 19-20)—even working with the new church to plant churches elsewhere.

SUMMARY

- Knowing the big picture is helpful for developing the strategy.
- The church-planting process can be conceptualized in six stages (pre-entry, entry, gospel, discipleship, church and leadership).
- The stages overlap at times—they are not mutually exclusive.
- The leadership stage runs parallel to the gospel, discipleship and church stages.
- The stages emphasize both reaching and teaching new believers.
- Phase-out forces the team to begin with its end in mind.
- The team should think of themselves as a scaffold—a temporary, supportive structure.

six

Planned Role Changes

•••

As the team moves from stage to stage, their responsibilities and activities change. This is absolutely necessary as the new disciples move through the sanctification process. In this chapter I will address one model of planned role changes for teams, and in chapter seven I will show the relationship between the role changes and the stages introduced in chapter five.

While figure 4 below provides a visual to assist us, we shouldn't assume that each role is as clearly defined as figure 4 makes it look. For example, though church planters do begin as learners, the reality is that they ought to remain learners throughout their labors. Also, the changes often merge into one another—hence the blurring of the boundaries in the figure. The team generally does not end one role on a certain date and then begin the next one the following morning. There is usually more of a tapering-off from one role and a slow transition into the next.

While the church-planting strategy (see chap. 11) should include plans to transition through these roles, your team should only progress to the next role as the Holy Spirit allows. The team should not allow time to drive the work but should follow the leadership of the Spirit, who oversees the timing of the ministry and its outworking in various contexts.

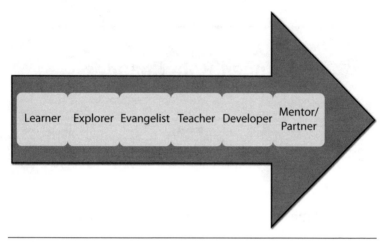

Figure 4. Planned role changes for teams

LEARNER

During this period, the team is learning all they can about them-selves and about the people they will serve. This role involves all the learning that occurs before the team arrives on the field and after they arrive as well. It involves the time necessary for team formation and development, understanding the context, language and cultural acquisition, strategy development and a host of other matters necessary to know for effective work to happen.

One of the things I want our church's church planters to do is to form teams from the members of our church. Once individuals and families form teams, they spend several months together getting to know one another. Every adult on the team goes through our twelve- to fifteen-month assessing and equipping process, which involves a couple of vision trips to the field. All of these things happen during the pre-entry stage. The team members un-derstand that their primary role at this point is to learn as much as they can as the Lord prepares them for the field.

EXPLORER

Closely connected to the role of learner is the role of explorer. During this period, the team enters into the community where they will be working and living. They scout out the land: observing the people, the marketplace, the public transportation and the way of life. Rather than learning via a book, computer or other people's stories, the team gains firsthand information about how to live and minister among the people.

While I was video chatting with one of our church's teams, one of the planters shared with me that there was a food court in an office complex near his apartment. One day he was there around noon and noticed that a large number of people who were eating were of the unreached people group his team was working to evangelize. He now regularly visits this location during lunchtime. If he had not been involved in his community as an explorer, he would not have been aware of this opportunity near his home.

Being an explorer may mean discarding your normal routine. It may involve late nights drinking tea or attending celebrations. I found an example of this in an email I received from a couple serving among the tens of thousands of Somalis in the Pacific Northwest.

Our language teacher invited my wife to attend a wedding with her this past weekend. It was a wonderful cultural experience for her. The wedding started around 10:00 p.m. and lasted until 3:00 a.m., so it was a late night and early morning but one full of loud music, beautiful clothes, dancing, smiles, laughter and yummy food. . . . It was such a joy to see a "hard" people be so happy, to see some unveiled and to see a divided people brought together. She also had the opportunity to drive a few women to the wedding and ended up becoming friends with one of them in particular. They have plans to hang out again soon, so please pray for this relationship to prosper.

Sometimes being an explorer means surveying the community for needs that can be met by the team. When I spoke with Nathan Graves, it was a stormy day in Albania. As the rain poured down and the thunder echoed across the sky, our video connection was surprisingly clear. Nathan and his family have been serving in the country for twenty-one years.

Nathan began his church-planting labors in the village of Krrabë. He started by simply surveying the people in an effort to better understand them. Recognizing a desire for English lessons, he began providing free classes that followed an Albanian Bible story.

People were required to hear the story before participating in the English lesson. Nathan found that though many were not familiar with the Bible, they were interested in learning about it.

These Bible stories were intentionally selected and followed a chronological approach, moving from creation to the gospel. For six months, about forty people came each week to hear the stories and learn English. Of this group, twenty-one people made a public profession of faith and were baptized in a local river.

EVANGELIST

Since biblical church planting is disciple making that results in new churches, and since making disciples begins with evangelism, during this period the team does the work of evangelism. They are sharing the gospel with the people, calling them to repentance and faith (Acts 20:21). The team should enter this role as soon as possible, sowing the gospel broadly among the people. One of the common characteristics among church-planting movements is that their origins can be traced to a widespread dissemination of the good news. Church-planting team members should expect to spend a great deal of time doing evangelism. If they are not willing to do so, then they should consider another ministry.

Andy and Josh are members of a church-planting team among Indian Hindus in New York. One day, while exploring and praying over his neighborhood, Andy struck up a conversation with "Sam," an Indian man sitting on the step outside his building. Noticing that Sam had an injured arm, Andy offered to pray for him. After prayer, Andy asked if he knew anything about Jesus. As Andy began to share his testimony with him, the man interrupted and said that he wanted to know more about Jesus but desired to hear about him in Gujarati. The team had just started learning Gujarati and were not proficient, but Andy was able to put Sam in touch with another believer who knew Gujarati, who was able to share the gospel in the Sam's heart language, with the result that Sam came to faith in Jesus.

Andy and Josh quickly followed up with Sam, gave him a Bible and began talking to him about the need to share his story with others. As soon as Andy got home from this meeting, he received a call from Sam's Hindu friend "Ted."

"Are you the person who gave Sam the book?"

"Yes," Andy replied.

"Can you come and tell me about Jesus, too?" Andy and Josh met with Ted shortly after this conversation, and he placed his faith in Jesus.

Wow! But this only happens if the team is doing the work of evangelism.

TEACHER

After people come to faith, it is important for the missionary team to begin teaching them both what to believe (doctrine) and how to follow (obedience). Teams must first reach people with the gospel, but then they must follow up by teaching them all that Jesus commanded (Matt 28:20).

Shortly after confessing Jesus, new believers should be taught about the reason they need to share their faith. They should identify someone in their acquaintance who needs to hear the message and be held accountable for sharing it in the next day or two. While the team will still be involved in evangelism and will be modeling it before the new believers—"imitate me just as I imitate Christ" (1 Cor 11:1 NLT)—they will be doing less and less evangelism as the new believers begin doing more and more. The team now begins to take on more of a teaching role.

There are many things that need to be taught to new believers. While contextual issues will necessitate specific teaching, in general I suggest the following matters that need to be covered:

- The gospel the new believers have received
- Their new nature and what it means to be a disciple
- The power of the Spirit in them
- Assurance of salvation
- God's Word and how to study it
- Prayer and fasting
- The hope of heaven and abundant life
- Baptism and the Lord's Supper
- The nature and function of the church
- Kingdom stewardship related to everything in our possession
- Disciple making and ministry (both local and global)

Nathan and Kari Shank challenge church planters to think in terms of short-term discipleship (what is needed for the first three months) and long-term discipleship (what is needed in the first three years). Drawing from George Patterson and Richard Scoggins's "seven commands of Christ," they advocate teaching the following for short-term discipleship:

- Repentance and faith
- Baptism
- Love (service, fellowship and worship)
- The Lord's Supper
- Giving
- Prayer
- The Great Commission[1]

A long-term discipleship strategy is also a must. By providing general teaching on the aforementioned topics, along with practical application, the team helps establish the new believers on a healthy foundation. But the new believers need to know not just right belief and practice but also *how* to study the Bible, *how* to rest in the Spirit and *how* to hold one another accountable and live in community. One of the best ways to do this is for the team to lead the new believers through a study of the books in the Bible.

God's Word is living and active. Over the years, as I have led congregations through books of the Bible, I have been amazed to see the Spirit and the Word work in conjunction with one another to challenge, convict, rebuke, encourage and exhort churches at just the right time, regardless of which book the church is studying. God's Word is relevant to any people in any context at any time.

Just as a parent is unable to answer all of the questions their children will face once they move out into the world, so the missionary team is unable to pass on to the new church everything they themselves have received since they first came to faith years ago. But like parents who provide their children with wisdom regarding how to think and how to live, the team gives the new believers a reproducible model and guidelines for being in community together. The team is to *empower* and *release* the new believers for their new life together, not try to do it for them.

The team—and the new believers—should understand that none of the biblical teachings and practices are meant to be lived out in isolation. A person cannot be a faithful follower of Jesus apart from a local expression of Jesus' universal body. There are no lone rangers in Christ. Personal spiritual disciplines should be taught, but they are never to be lived out apart from the covenant community.

The team must intentionally teach the new believers while simultaneously whetting their appetite for a self-identified community of disciples. Just as new believers need biblical teaching, they also need the fellowship of the local church. The team's strategy should include a designated date when the new believers are challenged to self-identify as a local church.

This target date should come after a time of teaching the new believers what it means to be a follower of Jesus and part of his church. If the team has been leading from God's Word and modeling the disciple's lifestyle regarding the importance of the local church in relation to the new nature, the Spirit, prayer and fasting, the hope of heaven and so on, then the new believers should see that being a local kingdom community is a matter of loving God with all of their heart, mind, soul and strength.

After a season of teaching, a simple challenge to the group can be expressed as follows:

You know all that we have been teaching you about following Jesus and the truth that none of us can follow him faithfully as individuals.

You have seen from God's Word—and not only from our words—that this is the case. As we have seen what the Scriptures teach about loving God, loving one another and loving those outside of his kingdom, we now want to challenge you as a group to identify yourselves as the local expression of Jesus' body.

Is the Holy Spirit calling you to unite together to live out the way of Jesus in this community as you serve God and make disciples of all nations? You have learned what the local church is and what it does. You are part of the universal body of Jesus, but you need to be part of his local body as well. Will you unite together before God and one another to be a local church?

Take time this week to pray, fast and discuss this matter among yourselves. Let's talk next week about what you sense the Spirit would have you do in relation to what he has been doing in your lives.

Once the group self-identifies as a local church, the church has been planted. It is a sacred moment. The new believers have entered into a covenant relationship with one another and with the Lord. Before this these believers were part of the universal body of Christ, but they were not a local church. They may have been a Bible study, an outreach group, a small group (see fig. 2, chap. 4) or even a community that worshiped, evangelized and fellowshiped together. But they did not identify themselves as a church. Although this self-identification may be seen as trivial, it is of great importance. If the group of new believers does not self-identify as a local church, then they will not think of themselves as a local church and thus will not live out the commands of Christ in community. Along with this commitment comes a greater accountability with one another, with other local churches and with God.

This is a very important moment in the church-planting process. It is very likely that if your team has been teaching and modeling what it means to follow Jesus and be part of his church, then the group will naturally follow your leadership to unite as a local church. The Spirit in them will make his will clear. It is very important that the people come to this understanding themselves—your team should not tell them that they are a church before they have had time to understand the Word, seek the Lord and process the implications for themselves.

Question: What if our group of new believers is especially small in number? Can they self-identify as a church?

Answer: Yes. There is no biblical prescription for the size of a church, other than the fact that fellowship cannot take place with one person. A church can be as much a New Testament church with five people as it can be with five thousand. A church is not defined by its size.

Question: Do we baptize the new believers before they self-identify as a local church or after?

Answer: In the New Testament, the act of baptism closely follows conversion (Mt 3:6; Mk 1:5; Acts 2:41; 8:12, 35-37; 9:17-18; 10:44-48; 16:14-15, 30-33). Baptism should occur as soon as possible after the regeneration of the Holy Spirit. Obviously, the team needs to take a moment to teach the new believers about the doctrine and practice of baptism. Part of the definition of a local church is that it is a baptized group of disciples of Jesus. If this is true, then in church-planting contexts baptism must occur before the church comes into existence. At this point there is no established church into which the new believers could be baptized—the Holy Spirit is in the process of birthing the local church as a fellowship into which future believers will be baptized. The founding members of the church will be baptized before they self-identify as the local church, even if both baptism and self-identification occur on the same day.

Question: What if the new believers decide not to self-identify as a church when the team challenges them to do so?

Answer: In this case they would need to be reminded or re-taught that no one is to follow Jesus apart from the local expression of his body. Your team should remind them that while you are laboring among them, even your team is part of a local church (wherever your sending church may be). If they are not willing to self-identify as a local church, then the team needs to assist the group in getting connected to another Bible-believing and teaching church. If no such church exists in the area, or if the group continues to refuse to be part of a local church, then the team should treat this as a matter of discipline that may prevent the team from continued ministry among the group.

DEVELOPER

In this role, the team works with the new church to appoint elders (that is, pastors). While it is to be expected that a time will come for deacons to be identified, pastoral leadership is primary and should be addressed as soon as possible. For both biblical and practical reasons, it is wise to have more than one elder, even if this means only two elders in the beginning. If the church is too small, or not enough people are qualified (make sure you define *qualified* according to Scripture), then one elder will have to suffice for the time being.

The team should teach the church about the role and office of the elder by examining the biblical passages that address pastors. The church should be challenged with the question, "Now that we have examined the biblical teachings, what should pastoral ministry look like in this church family?" The church should consider the application of biblical teaching in its context, rather than the missionary team's preference.

While the team may have already identified potential elders, they should seek the wisdom of the church in this process. The team's influence during this time is very important, but the church needs to recognize its responsibility to be self-governing and to make its own decisions in light of the Word and guidance of the Spirit (Acts 20:28). This new church has just as much of the Holy Spirit as the team and may well discern things about certain people among them that are unknown to the team.

The church should be led in a time of prayer and fasting for the appointment of pastoral leadership. After examining some potential elders who meet the biblical requirements, the candidates should be extended an invitation from the church to serve as the elders. If they accept this calling, a time of prayer, laying on of hands by the team and the church and possibly a challenge to the new pastors from the team should mark this wonderful occasion.

After this the team will transition to the next role and spend more of their time with the pastors and less with the church.

Question: Shouldn't these elders be ordained?

Answer: There is little in the Bible to support much of the ordination processes that have developed over church history. While such traditions are not necessarily bad practices, they are largely unnecessary. Examining Spirit-filled people according to the biblical requirements (both of lifestyle and of belief), prayer and laying on of hands by the church as a sign of affirmation and call to the church for service is sufficient to begin pastoral ministry.

Question: Is the plant-and-pastor model wrong? I want to plant and pastor a church.

Answer: No. It is not wrong. If God has called you to this ministry, then go for it! However, the plant-and-pastor model should be the *exception* and not the *expectation* when it comes to church planting. The more frequent biblical model is that the missionary team will do apostolic work and then raise up pastors from the new churches. If your desire is to plant and pastor, it is likely that your calling is to the pastorate and not to missionary service. If this is the case, then you should have a group of long-standing kingdom citizens with you from the beginning of the work. You need to plant an instant church with them and lead them to make disciples, both locally and globally. If you are called to pastor, then you need to begin by pastoring a church to be on mission rather than doing apostolic work yourself. Then you should lead that church to send out apostolic teams—remembering that the church does not have to reproduce the model you used to plant that church.

MENTOR/PARTNER

This final role is likely to last indefinitely. The team transitions from being engaged in the pastoral aspects of the ministry to mentoring and equipping the new pastors from the churches themselves. The team spends less time with the church and more time with the pastors so that these new leaders can take over the shepherding of the church.

Jesus sent his Spirit. Paul returned to visit the churches he had planted, wrote letters to them and sent others to visit them in his place. With these examples as their model, the missionary team never abandons the churches they plant. Though the team will eventually be physically absent from the church, they are to remain in partnership with the church and its leaders. Social media, video chat, texting and other technologies—as well as safe and rapid air travel—have made such relationships easier than ever to maintain.

In the New Testament we read of churches who partnered with Paul for the advancement of the gospel to unreached peoples and other ministry opportunities (Rom 15:24; Phil 4:14-19). In this role the team colabors with the new church to make disciples and plant churches among unreached peoples—maybe down the street, maybe across the world. Just as the new churches were on Paul's heart and mind (2 Cor 2:4; 11:28; 1 Thess 2:17-20), the team should continue to be concerned about the welfare of the church. It should take advantage of opportunities to visit, write and even send representatives to assist with particular needs and encourage them in the faith (1 Thess 3:2). The team should continue to assist the pastors in their development as leaders in spiritual formation, doctrine and practical ministry. In this role the team is able to provide some outside accountability to the pastors, and ultimately the whole church.

Question: In chapter five, you talked about the phase-out thread running through all the stages of church planting. Isn't phase-out abandoning the new churches?

Answer: No. Absolutely not. Phase-out involves ongoing relationships. It is similar to Jesus preparing his disciples for his departure and the coming of the Spirit and to Paul's ongoing followup with the churches he planted. Phase-out is about equipping and releasing churches for ministry (Eph 4:11-12) and not allowing them to be dependent on the team for doing ministry.

Question: Didn't Paul leave to work in other areas because persecution prevented him from staying?

Answer: Yes, sometimes. This is clearly seen in the first and second missionary journeys, though Paul would return to visit the churches in those areas. Sometimes he stayed (at the Lord's command) in the face of hostility (Acts 18:9-10). Other times he could have stayed but was moved by the Spirit to work elsewhere (Acts 20:36-38). He was driven by a desire to evangelize the unreached (Rom 15:19-21).

Question: Will every team pass through all six roles?

Answer: These roles are not strictly linear. They bleed together at multiple points. The transition of the team through the different roles will depend on what the Spirit is doing in that specific context. It is possible that a team may spend their entire ministry (or their entire lives) doing evangelism. Church history has shown this to be the case in some situations. As long as a team is faithful to the Lord and wise about their strategy and methods, then they are successful in the kingdom—even if they never see a church planted. But all church-planting teams should intentionally develop their strategies with planned role changes in mind. If they enter a mission field believing that a church will never be planted in their lifetime, then it is unlikely that their prayers, methods and daily lives will be directed toward church planting.

Table 1. Team roles with primary tasks

Role	Primary Task
Learner	Develop team and strategy
Explorer	Connect with the people
Evangelist	Make disciples through evangelism
Teacher	Baptize, lead group to self-identify as a church, teach doctrine and obedience
Developer	Appoint elders
Mentor/Partner	Train elders and partner for new work

SUMMARY

Your team should move through planned role changes with intentionality but only as the Spirit allows. While there is an urgency to take the gospel to all people, evangelism should never happen at the expense of discipleship and church health. The same apostle who desired that the Word should "speed ahead and be honored" (2 Thess 3:1) also believed in teaching the "whole counsel of God"

(Acts 20:27). Your team is not commanded to plant a church but to make disciples who will bear fruit (John 15:16) through a local expression of the body of Christ. Your strategy should reflect such changes. These transitions allow your team to equip and empower the new churches and their pastors (Eph 4:11-12) even as they transition to new mission fields in partnership with the new church. Table 1 illustrates the church-planter roles and the corresponding primary task for each.

seven

Church Multiplication Cycle

•••

I've never enjoyed working on jigsaw puzzles—too many pieces to connect together. I remember seeing a thousand-piece puzzle spread across a card table as a child and watching a relative take a large amount of time to work on the project. Corner pieces were selected first, followed by the border pieces. Next, small sections of the puzzle (a pond, then a mountain) would be worked on before bringing all of the sections together.

In this chapter, I hope to take the contents of the two previous chapters—church-planting stages and roles—and show how they fit together. Hopefully this will help you understand the big picture of the church-planting process, as well as demonstrate that this process is not as complicated as it may seem.

Church-planting teams with a heart for the nations will not be satisfied with the birth of one church. They understand that once they have entered into the mentor/partner role much work still remains, including carrying on the disciple-making process elsewhere (maybe even among a different unreached people).

The Church Multiplication Cycle notes that the process of making disciples and planting churches will continue until the Lord's return. The Church Multiplication Cycle is diagrammed in figure 5 below. As with the stages and roles, the cycle should not be seen as a neat linear process. Stages blur together and the transition from role to role is never cut and dried. For example, the team will always be in the learner role, not just when they begin their work. Also, church-planting teams should be encouraged to share the gospel as soon as possible, though figure 4 (chap. 6) places it *after* the explorer role. Baptism and teaching new disciples fundamentals are likely to occur simultaneously, or baptism may happen moments following conversion. Though the team may enter the discipleship stage (see chap. 5) and thus spend more time teaching, they will continue to share the gospel.

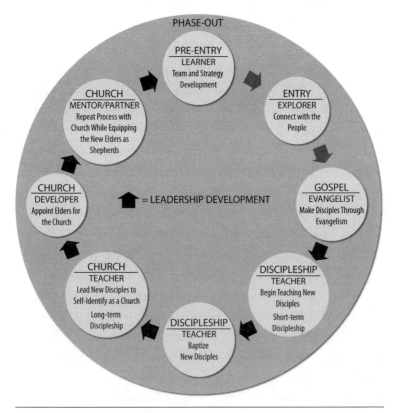

Figure 5. Church multiplication cycle

In this cycle (which begins at the twelve o'clock position), the team begins their work as learners in the pre-entry stage. Everything they do before beginning work in the field is placed in this circle. While their primary activities are related to team and strategy development, other activities include, but are not limited to: training, language learning, preparing for their move, vision trips, finding a place to live, obtaining employment in the new community, choosing prayer partners and so on.

Moving clockwise through the cycle, the team arrives on the field but still has not started to engage in depth with the people. They are trying to learn as much as they can through the sights, sounds and smells of the community. Although the team has spent time learning about the people and community from afar, now they are on the ground learning through firsthand experience.

As soon as possible, the team should be sowing the gospel seed broadly. Since biblical church planting is evangelism that results in new churches, the team does not move on to the role of teacher until people come to faith in Jesus. I have heard of church planters who have spent their entire ministries in the role of evangelist and others who have seen people come to faith within a few months of their arrival on the field. Remaining faithful to the Lord's calling on their lives while working hard to preach a contextualized message that the people can understand is key to the work. While many teams will see disciples made, others called to very resistant soils may never see conversions. Some will only plant and water, but God alone provides the growth (1 Cor 3:5-6). Teams can rest in this truth.

Though the team may find themselves in the evangelism stage for a long time, the discipleship and church stages include the majority of the activities of the cycle. During this time, the team functions primarily as teachers, developers and mentor/partners. The Great Commission is more than seeing people make a profession of faith in Jesus. The team is also called to teach new believers and churches what it means to be and make disciples.

Before the cycle is repeated, the team is to be involved in the appointment and equipping of new pastors for the church. During the role of mentor/partner, the team either continues the church-planting process elsewhere as the new church begins their own church-planting efforts, or the team colabors with the new church in sending a new team together to plant churches.

As shown in figure 5, the phase-out thread (see chap. 5) is woven throughout the process. The team must keep these planned role changes in mind from pre-entry all the way up until they begin work in a new community. The strategy developed (chap. 11) reflects this thinking as the team grows less directly involved in the ministry, and the leadership is handed over to the new church.

Question: If our team is to begin another work elsewhere, does this mean that a church-planting team has to move from location to location every time a church is planted?

Answer: Not necessarily. Clearly, the Spirit sometimes does lead a team to a different location. We see this throughout the Scriptures. But the Spirit may lead the team to begin work among a different people in the same location. Given the size of contemporary urban contexts, it is very possible for a team to spend many years in one location, planting multiple churches among unreached peoples.

SUMMARY

- The Church Multiplication Cycle notes that the process of making disciples and planting churches will continue until the Lord's return.

- Though the Cycle is diagrammed in a linear fashion, transitions on the field are not so cut and dried.

- The Cycle shows the connections between the stages, roles and primary tasks of the team.

- While the team will be involved in many activities at any given moment, knowing their primary task for each role will give them focus and direction in the field.

eight

Methods

•••

While I have never been an avid fisherman, I do enjoy fishing. Over the years I have spent a good deal of time—both as a kid and with my own kids—on the banks of ponds and lakes and fishing from boats. Once I traveled an hour into the Atlantic to go deep-sea fishing. I've never been fly fishing, though I have wanted to. I've never trawled with a net either, or gone after swordfish, shrimp or crabs. Though my experience of fishing is limited, one thing I do know is that there are many different ways to fish.

Some of these methods involve standing on land, while others require a boat. Still others involve wading out in a stream. Some require a very heavy line, while others call for a lightweight line. Floaters are used in some situations but are problematic in others. Small hooks are necessary for certain kinds of fish, huge hooks for others.

Similarly, the methods used in church planting are the means to accomplish the desired result—making a catch. And while it is important to understand the big picture (such as the Church Multiplication Cycle), church-planting teams use methods to accomplish their desired result of making disciples and planting churches. Just as fishermen are no strangers to methods, church planters should be familiar with different approaches too.

Jeff serves as a church-planting catalyst, helping to equip and mobilize churches and church-planting teams. Many of these teams serve in the United States among unreached people groups from Saudi Arabia, Yemen, Burma, Bangladesh, Nepal and Egypt.

I asked Jeff about the methods used among the Muslim groups. He began by summarizing their overall approach. "We want to use simple evangelism and church-planting methods that are transferable to the new believers and churches and are easily reproducible across their social networks."

Talking specifics, Jeff said, "We try to get to the gospel message as soon as we can in our interaction with others. That's where the power is found. We begin having many spiritual conversations with others and then invite them to continue our conversations through an eleven-week discovery Bible study that is customized to the person's religious background. For example, we use a study tool called 'The Prophet' with our Muslim friends, which begins with creation and continues to the birth of the church. This study particularly addresses matters related to shame and fear—significant issues in many Muslim cultures."

The Spirit cannot be limited to a timeline, and not everyone's journey to faith is the same. Even so, Jeff mentioned that church planters using this method are seeing Muslims come to faith after about a three-month period and be baptized shortly thereafter, and are reporting new churches after two years.

Jeff stressed the importance of church planters teaching a healthy ecclesiology to the new believers. Shortly after people come to faith, the team teaches them about persecution and begins to cast a vision for them to be a local church. Biblical teaching on the nature and purpose of the church follows, and the new small group usually comes to the conclusion that the Spirit has led them to become a local expression of the body of Christ.

GUIDELINES FOR CHURCH-PLANTING METHODOLOGY

Methods are the how-to components of the strategy (chap. 11)—
some people refer to them as tactics. Until the team applies
methods to the field, the desired result exists only in theory. In this
chapter I will share a few guidelines that teams should keep in
mind as they determine their methods.

Methods should be biblical. The methods used in the Church
Multiplication Cycle must be rooted in Scripture. While a "whatever
it takes" attitude to reach people with the gospel sounds good, it can
result in a team that embraces unhealthy methods just because they
produce results. Methods must never diminish the gospel, what it
means to be a disciple or what it means to be the church.

Methods should be reproducible. The methods used by a church-
planting team serve as a model to the people group. While complex
and nuanced methods may be needed at times to reach people and
plant churches, this should not be the norm. People reproduce
what they know, and they know what is modeled for them. Your
team should model methods that are simple enough for the people
to reproduce when they in turn share the gospel and plant churches.

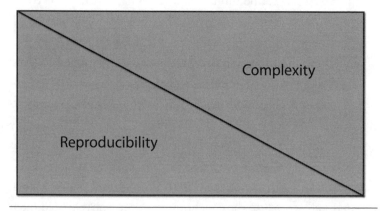

Figure 6. Reproducibility potential guide

The Reproducibility Potential Guide (fig. 6) shows there is generally an inverse relationship between complex methods and the potential for the gospel to spread among the people as they labor to plant churches in their turn. The more complex the team's methods, the more difficult it will be for the church to reproduce the disciple-making and church-planting methods used to reach them. The best way to tell whether a method is too complex is to get to know the people well. Pray for wisdom and the Spirit's leadership. What is simple in one society is complex in another. The learner and explorer roles will help the team discern their methods.

Your team should desire that new believers become "imitators of us and of the Lord," and thus "an example to all the believers," and that their faith spreads rapidly and with honor (1 Thess 1:6-8; 2 Thess 3:1).

Methods should be ethical. As followers of Jesus we should never use methods that compromise our integrity. Every aspect of our lives should be above reproach (1 Tim 3:2). Regardless of the outcome, coercion, deception, threats and manipulation have no place in the methods used by church planters.

Methods should avoid paternalism. Paternalism is the belief that the team knows what is best for the people. For much of the last two hundred years of Protestant missionary history, Western missionaries believed that other societies were uncivilized and ignorant. Teams were sent out to establish mission stations and plant churches that were organized and led just like their Western counterparts. New believers did not have the education of the missionaries, so it was assumed that they could not lead churches like churches ought to be led. The result was that new believers were taught that the Western way was the biblical way, and since they were unable to afford or oversee such complex structures or teach in the same style, they had to be dependent on outsiders.

While experience and wisdom are very important, there is no call for the team to create an unhealthy dependency among new believers. Church history is filled with examples of church-planting teams using methods that required the new churches to be dependent on the teams for evangelism, teaching, ministry, leadership and so on. Rather than using methods that equipped and released the new churches, the teams restricted the churches to what they thought best based on their own cultural traditions. You wouldn't fit a small child with a size fifteen shoe and then insist to the child that it fits! But church planters often create structures that are unsuited to the culture they're working in and then insist that these structures are the biblical norm. No wonder they get frustrated when the people can't sustain the church over a period of time!

As much as possible, your team should use methods that teach people to be dependent on the Holy Spirit, God's Word, one another and their pastoral leaders. The phase-out thread requires that the methods used allow the team to raise up new churches as co-laborers in the gospel ministry—not create codependency.

Methods should manifest Christ-sustained abilities. From the moment a church is planted, it needs to manifest at least seven abilities. Charles Brock refers to these classic "self-" terms as "Christ-sustained abilities" to avoid confusing them with an ungodly self-sufficiency.[1] The methods your team uses should help people become:

- Self-identifying: they should identify as a local expression of the body of Christ.

- Self-supporting: they should have all of the financial and human resources needed to be and function as a local church.

- Self-governing: with God's Word, their elders and a Spirit-filled body, they should be able to make their own decisions regarding life and ministry.

- Self-propagating: as the Spirit leads them, they should be able to carry out the Great Commission in their local and global contexts.

- Self-expressing: without deviating from the biblical guidelines for worship, they should be able to express themselves in ways they believe to be appropriate to their cultural context.

- Self-teaching: the people should be able to exhort, rebuke, encourage and instruct one another according to God's Word as the Spirit leads, equips and gifts them.

- Self-theologizing: relying on God's Word, the indwelling Spirit and one another for discernment and accountability, they should be able to apply biblical truths to their unique cultural context.

Question: How is a new church to manifest these abilities so quickly after its birth?

Answer: These abilities come from the Spirit's power within. Do not read too much into them. What the church is able to do today is likely to be different five years from now. For example, in some contexts self-supporting means having a multi-million dollar budget with full-time employees; it can also mean simply being able to make ten photocopies of some material using the church's money. Self-governing could mean conducting business meetings with *Robert's Rules of Order* for proper parliamentary procedure; it could also mean simply being able to decide where the church will meet for its first worship gathering. Self-theologizing could mean being able to write a systematic theology, or it could mean simply answering the question, "How do we apply this biblical teaching about marriage to our context?" The church will grow and develop in these abilities, but it is able to manifest them in some sense from day one.

Methods should not be used if they hinder the church from manifesting these abilities. As much as possible, every decision

made by your team should be assessed according to the Reproducibility Potential Guide (see fig. 6).

For example, if during the evangelism stage unbelievers ask,
"Where should we meet to study about Jesus?" an appropriate team
response is: "Where do you want to meet?" Allowing them to make
such decisions, even before they come to faith, teaches them to be
self-governing.

Or suppose new believers ask the team: "What should we do next
week when we meet?" A good answer from the team would be: "Let's
look at Acts 2:42-47 and consider what the church in Jerusalem did
when it gathered." This approach demonstrates that the new believers
can be self-teaching and self-theologizing as they look to God's
Word for the answers, not the team. Most of us are quick to give
answers, but in the discipleship stage (see fig. 3, chap. 5) it is important
that the team models the truth that God's Word is the source for the
answers to such questions.

For example, after studying a passage in the Psalms, your team
could ask: "As we have seen in the Bible, music and singing were an
important part of worshiping God. How do you think we should
apply this truth to your weekly gathering?" Such questions teach the
new community to be self-expressing. Contrast this with simply
telling the new believers, "The church is a worshipping community
with psalms, hymns and spiritual songs, so next week we'll bring a
guitar and some songs to sing."

Continuing with this example, someone from the group may say
to the team, "We should have some music and sing to God! But none
of us can play an instrument. Will you play for us?" Since the team is
teaching the new believers to be self-supporting—even before the
church is actually planted—one response could be: "Yes, it would be
great to have some music and sing to God. However, even though
you are unable to play an instrument, you can sing a cappella."

While the team will always believe they are able to do things better than the new believers (and they may be right), they must refrain from what is expected in their church's culture. If the team makes all the decision for the group, plans the worship gatherings, plays the music, handles any tithes and offerings, prints worship guides and so on, the people will draw conclusions that will hinder the multiplication of disciples and churches:

- "Wow! So this is what it means to do it right and please God!"

- "There is no way we could ever do that. Look at how gifted, talented and equipped they are."

- "They will have to do it for us because we want to do it right and be pleasing to God."

Methods matter a great deal. Your team should be able to say to the new believers, "Be imitators of me, as I am of Christ" in life and doctrine (1 Cor 11:1; also 2 Tim 3:10; Heb 13:7). If you team is using methods that are difficult for the people to own and apply, then you are not being a wise steward of the opportunity the Spirit has set before you. Remember, your team is not trying to attract long-term kingdom citizens but to evangelize a people, make disciples, start a small group, lead the group to self-identify as a church and then appoint pastors with that church.

There are many methods for planting churches—some better than others. When missionary teams say they have the unevangelized people of the world in mind, do their methods reflect that thinking?

SUMMARY

We'll summarize this chapter with some questions for your team to discuss as you consider methods for making disciples and planting churches.

- How will your team connect with people?

- How will your team share the gospel as widely and as soon as possible?

- How will your team begin teaching new believers in community (1) to be disciples of Jesus, (2) to share the Word with others, (3) to practice biblical community, (4) to study and teach the Word to one another and (5) to serve the world both locally and globally?

- How will your team incorporate culturally appropriate elements into gatherings as you lead the new believers toward their identity as a church?

  - Will you lead them to have a meal together?

  - Will you lead them to incorporate music in a time of praise?

  - Will you have corporate sharing and prayer times?

  - Will you allow for them to read publicly from the Word (assuming they are literate)?

  - Will you encourage public testimonies to God's grace?

  - Will you challenge them to collect an offering (appropriate to their economy) for mission and ministry to one another and for the poor, orphans, widows, church planters and so on? How will they collect and distribute it?

- What other questions should your team consider?

nine

Where to Begin?

•••

The world is a big place. At the time of this writing, the global population is about seven billion. Where should the team begin their kingdom labors?

All disciple-making and church-planting activities involve crossing cultures to some degree. Even when a team serves people from their own ethnic group and speaks the same language, they still have to cross over from the kingdom of light and communicate the gospel in the kingdom of darkness. This may be a small cultural gap, but it requires crossing into another way of thought and life nonetheless.

Some teams need to serve where the cultural gap is not too wide. Given the team's calling, the people's need and receptivity levels (see fig. 7 below) and the personal characteristics, abilities, interests and passions of the team, near-culture church planting is the best fit for them. However, the greatest need—in the West and around the world—is for teams to engage in disciple-making labors that require engaging cultures that are significantly different from the team.

Regarding the global realities and the Great Commission, we know that

• Jesus has already told us to make disciples of all peoples.

• At the time of this writing, there are over six thousand unreached people groups in the world (an unreached people group is defined here as a people group that is less than 2 percent evangelical).

- There are at least 360 unreached people groups in the United States and at least 180 in Canada.

- Over three thousand people groups in the world are considered *both* unreached *and* unengaged (less than 2 percent evangelical and no evangelicals are serving among them with a church-planting strategy).

- Most of the global missionary activity by evangelicals is among reached people groups.

- Most of the church-planting activity in North America is among reached people groups.[1]

Given these realities, church-planting teams should use the following guidelines to help them decide where to begin their labors.

GUIDELINE 1: ASSUME THE GREAT COMMISSION

Since Jesus has already given the command to make disciples of all nations, any unengaged and unreached people group should receive priority, wherever they exist in the world. Next to unengaged-unreached people groups, unreached people groups should be the second priority. Clearly the greatest needs for disciple making and church multiplication exist outside of the West, but many unengaged-unreached and unreached people groups can be found in the West, too.

One Saturday in Birmingham, Alabama, forty members of The Church at Brook Hills spent four hours in the city attempting to identify the people groups living among us. Though the population of our city is over one million people, we identified thirty-six different groups on that day! We encountered people from Yemen,

Vietnam, India, Nepal, China, Saudi Arabia, Bhutan and Mexico. While Birmingham is one of the most evangelical cities in the most evangelical state in the country, most of these groups were unreached. And most of those identified as unreached were not being engaged by anyone in our city. The result of this simple excursion into our community was the formation of several church-planting teams who would focus on the unreached people groups in Birmingham.

GUIDELINE 2: THERE IS A SPECIFIC CALLING TO HARD SOIL

The call to make disciples is a call with a results-oriented expectation. However, some teams will receive a specific leading by the Spirit to serve in a resistant soil. They will spend their ministries like Ezekiel or Jeremiah, with very few tangible results when it comes to disciples made and churches planted. In the past church planters have labored among some unreached people groups for twenty, thirty or forty years before the first person came to faith in Jesus. It was thirty-three years after missionaries first brought the gospel to the Ao people of Nagaland that the first church was planted. Many people in the world will only be reached if teams are willing to labor among them for long periods of time. If your team has received a specific leading from the Lord to such a people, then your team must be faithful to the work of the Spirit. It would be a sin to abandon such a mission to serve among a more receptive people.

Your team should not feel any embarrassment about serving among resistant people or feel inferior to teams who labor among more receptive people. Make sure your team does not make unhealthy comparisons with teams in areas where many people are coming to faith. Be faithful wherever the Spirit places you. Remember Jesus' words: "So you also, when you have done all that you were commanded, say, 'We are unworthy servants; we have only done what was our duty'" (Lk 17:10). Take comfort in your calling to hard soil, knowing that your labor in the Lord is never in vain (1 Cor 15:58) and that your team is exactly where they should be at this moment in time.

GUIDELINE 3: CONSIDER NEED *AND* RECEPTIVITY

If your team has not received a specific leading from the Spirit to a highly resistant people, they should consider the matters of both need and receptivity. The Great Commission is a given. Where would your team be the best stewards of the resources they have been given? Need corresponds to how many followers of Jesus there are in a given people group. Receptivity corresponds to how people groups respond when the gospel is shared in contextually appropriate ways. Do not assume that just because a group is unreached or unengaged-unreached they will be resistant to the gospel.

In *Discovering Church Planting* I note that it is helpful to think in terms of four general fields that may relate to any people group anywhere in the world.[2] Each of these fields is categorized by the percent of evangelicals already present and the people's response to

RECEPTIVITY

		High	Low
NEED	High	Priority 1	Priority 2
	Low	Priority 3	Priority 4

Figure 7. Receptivity-need guide

the gospel. Keep in mind that these fields are *only a guide*, not a law. Figure 7 provides a visual to help teams as they consider need and receptivity. Your team should consider working first among those who would be categorized as priority 1 or priority 2.

If a people group is less than 2 percent evangelical, missiologists categorize them as unreached. Large concentrations of such people are found throughout the world (including North America), and with international migration, many of these unreached (and unengaged-unreached) people groups can be found living in areas where there are large concentrations of believers from other people groups.

Jason Williams is a friend of mine who serves among the largest Afghan population in the United States. He shared with me that the need for the gospel was a crucial part of his call to the Afghan people living in the San Francisco Bay Area.

"I went to them even though it was uncomfortable, instead of making them coming to me," Jason said. While living in South Carolina, Jason heard of the large Afghan population living near San Francisco. Though he knew little about the people, he saw their need and moved to "Little Kabul." He started meeting Afghan people in the community, sharing tea and coffee with them, and inviting them into his home to share his life—and the gospel— with them. In 2006 Jason even traveled to Afghanistan, using the social networks of the people he knew from his own community. This brought opportunities for him to share the good news with friends and family members of those living back in California.

While attending a conference in the United States, Omed, an Afghan believer, heard Jason share about his work in California. Later, Omed had a dream in which he was challenged to move to the Bay Area to share the gospel and plant churches among his own people. After Omed teamed up with Jason and with a Korean church in the area, a few Afghan people came to faith and a church was planted from the harvest field.

The work was not easy. Jason told me, "It was messy. But we went and trusted God to provide." And it all began when Jason heard of the need.

When considering need, teams should find out the percentage of the population who are followers of Jesus and the number of evangelical churches present for the people group. In the urban context, is there at least one church present for every one thousand people (with the church comprising at least one hundred members)? In the rural context, is there at least one church present for every five hundred people (with the church comprising at least fifty members)? Again, these numbers are only a general guide, but they are based on research and missiological thought.[3]

Receptivity relates to the people's response to the team and to the gospel when it is presented in a culturally relevant way. Though all unbelievers are dead in their trespasses and sins (Eph 2:1), the reactions of people to the gospel vary. Some are very resistant, even hostile, to the message (and the messengers). Some people are apathetic. Others are like the Philippian jailer, who immediately asked, "What must I do to be saved?" (Acts 16:30).

Unless the team is led to work among more resistant people (priority 2), they should work among people where the Spirit has already been working to ripen the field for harvest (priority 1). The gospel travels faster and farther and produces fruit more rapidly in places where people are more receptive to its message. There are varying degrees of response among any people—including the most hostile to the gospel. Not every individual manifests the same degree of receptivity. Even if the team is called to a more resistant people, they should seek to work among those who are more receptive among the resistant. (For more information on receptivity and where to begin, see chapters ten and eleven in *Discovering Church Planting*, and chapters nineteen and twenty in Terry and Payne, *Developing a Strategy for Missions*.[4])

Question: How can you tell whether a people is receptive to the gospel?

Answer: Share the gospel with them through a contextually appropriate method and pay attention to their response. After a time of sharing with different people across the group, the team will begin to develop an understanding of the receptivity level of the people. In areas where there are churches or other church-planting teams working among the people group, teams can ask, "Are others observing people coming into the kingdom?"

Question: If you give priority to receptive people, does that mean that the unreached and unengaged-unreached will never have church-planting teams working among them? Won't teams tend to go only to those groups who are more reached?

Answer: No. Do not assume that just because a people is either unreached or unengaged-unreached that they are highly resistant to the gospel. They may be very receptive. Also, do not assume that the more reached a people group is, the more receptive they will be. Over time, they may have become more apathetic to the gospel.

Question: My team is serving among a people who are not very receptive to the gospel. Should we leave and serve elsewhere among a more receptive people?

Answer: This is a question your team should answer after seeking the Lord and talking with the leadership of your sending church. Jesus departed regions when the people refused his message (Mk 5:17-18). He instructed the Twelve and the seventy-two to depart towns in which the people were resistant (Mt 10:14; Lk 9:5; 10:10-11). When Paul and Barnabas experienced resistance from the Jews in

Antioch in Pisidia, they devoted their efforts to the more receptive Gentiles (Acts 13:46-52). In Corinth, Paul "shook out his garments" and turned his effort to the Gentiles (Acts 18:1-11).

While there are examples in Scripture of teams departing from one location to serve in another because of the people's resistance to the message, there is no easy answer to this question. If wisdom from God and counsel from other believers indicate that it is time to move along, and if the Spirit provides a sense of peace and an opportunity to labor among a different people, then it may be time to make a transition. However, some people will only be reached by teams willing to labor among them for many years before seeing any real fruit. In the history of church-planting movements, great awakenings and widespread multiplication of churches have often occurred only after decades of prayer, fasting and sowing the seed.

Question: Can the receptivity-need guide be used among resistant peoples?

Answer: Absolutely! It should be used by a team working in hard soil. The guide is not an absolute, since no people group can be completely categorized into simple "high receptivity" or "low receptivity" boxes. A spectrum of receptivity exists among all people groups, including those who are the least receptive. Teams serving among such people groups should ask, "Who among this people group are less resistant to the gospel than the majority?" While such people may still be a long way from asking the Philippian jailer's question, they are not as resistant as others from among their people group. As a general guide, once those people are located, the team should begin with them.

SUMMARY

The apostolic nature of church-planting teams requires that they think and function as missionaries. The greatest need in both the

Western world and the Majority World is for church-planting teams to make significant cultural leaps in order to reach unreached and unengaged-unreached peoples. Until this happens, many peoples of the world will remain separated from God.

Teams should prayerfully consider where they should begin their labors. Time should be spent in fasting and prayer, seeking the Spirit's guidance. Obviously the team should assume the Great Commission and then consider whether the Spirit is prompting them to work among a resistant people.

The concepts of need and receptivity should be considered when deciding where to begin. Give utmost priority to the most needy and receptive people. A second priority is people who are the most needy but have a low receptivity level. Even for teams with a specific calling to a highly resistant people, the receptivity-need guide can provide guidance regarding where to begin.

ten

Pastoral Development

•••

Your church-planting team has the opportunity to establish new churches on a healthy foundation, especially when it comes to the area of leadership.

One of the most important parts of the Church Multiplication Cycle (see fig. 5, chap. 7) is the appointment of elders for a local church. Paul and Barnabas considered this act to be so important that it was the last thing they did among the churches before returning to Antioch (Acts 14:23). Paul also left Titus on Crete so that he "might put what remained into order, and appoint elders in every town as I directed you" (Tit 1:5). While a church can be planted without elders in place, elders should be raised up as soon as possible. (For more information on leadership development and church planting, see chapter eight in *Discovering Church Planting*.)

DO NOT DEVIATE FROM BIBLICAL EXPECTATIONS

The Bible has delineated the requirements and expectations for those who oversee churches. Your team must hold to these and not deviate from them. The following passages will assist you in your study:

- Acts 20:28-35
- Ephesians 4:11-12

- 1 Timothy 3:1-7; 5:17-19
- Titus 1:5-9
- 1 Peter 5:1-4

As a team, prayerfully consider who among the new believers is eligible to serve in this leadership capacity. Using the Bible, explain to the church that the kingdom ethic requires elders to be in place to shepherd the flock. Emphasis should be placed on the servant nature of this role—showing how such leaders are to display Jesus in their lives, in their families and in their responsibilities of leading, teaching, caring and guarding the church. The church should understand that while such leaders are worthy of double honor (1 Tim 5:17) and will be judged with greater strictness (Jas 3:1), they are ordinary people—just like the rest of the church. They should not be elevated to a higher pedestal than the Bible allows. Your team should do nothing to create a two-tiered division in the church between clergy and laity.

Though Paul, Barnabas and Titus were involved in appointing elders for the churches, they understood that it was the Holy Spirit who made such people overseers (Acts 20:28). Since the Scriptures imply that there should be multiple elders for each church, your team should work with the church to select at least two leaders to serve in this capacity. If two cannot be found, start with one, with the expectation that more will be appointed in the future.

While your team should use its influence to put the first elders in place, allow the church to make the decision. Such decision-making allows them to be self-governing as they listen to the Spirit and the Word, and it shows that your team is treating them as colaborers in the mission, rather than being paternalistic. Once the people who have been chosen have agreed to serve in this capacity, the church—not the team—should extend the call to them to be elders.

DEVIATE FROM CULTURAL REQUIREMENTS

No team is culturally neutral. Everyone is biased by their traditions and cultural expectations. However, your team should constantly evaluate how much of your expectations for the new pastors are governed by the Scriptures and how much comes from your own cultural preferences.

While such cultural requirements may not be inherently wrong, they can hinder the sanctification of the church, the spread of the gospel and the multiplication of churches. Just because this or that expectation worked well in your own experience or in your home church does not necessarily mean it will be healthy for this new church.

Church history is full of examples of church planters from the West planting churches in Majority World countries and expecting their pastors to live up to the educational and cultural standards established over centuries back home. The result? Many of the churches could not provide their own elders, so missionaries from outside the people group had to step in. For those churches that were able to provide such people from among themselves, the potential elders had to go through years of education and training before they could serve according to the standard set by the missionaries' tradition.

Cultural requirements are also found among new believers, particularly when they form new churches in post-Christianized contexts. Even though they themselves are new in the faith, they have learned from their observations of Christians over the years that pastors look and act in a certain way. As with the team's cultural expectations, such expectations may be healthy or unhealthy. If they are unhealthy, the team should guide the church to a biblical understanding and then help them think through what such leadership should look like in their own context. Jesus often used the formula, "You have heard it was said . . . but I tell you . . ." Follow this model when it is necessary to correct new believers whose minds have been distorted by unhealthy Christian examples.

MANIFEST MISSIONARY FAITH

One of the most shocking passages in the Bible is Acts 20:17-38—Paul's address to the Ephesian elders. Why? Imagine having just planted a church in a place with great satanic forces at play and much opposition from the unbelievers. Former pagan magicians are now church members. Now imagine getting in a boat and setting sail for Jerusalem, knowing that evil is coming to attempt to destroy the church and that you will never see these believers again. If he knew what was about to happen to these new believers, why didn't Paul stay? That's shocking!

Paul spent just three years in Ephesus—a polytheistic, demonic context (Acts 19). Wanting to get to Jerusalem for the day of Pentecost (Acts 20:16), he intentionally avoided returning to visit the Ephesian church and instead called for the elders to meet him at Miletus (vv. 15-17).

Paul's address reveals not only details of his labor in Ephesus but also startling insights into the future. He notes that the Spirit has constrained him to go to Jerusalem (v. 22), and that after he leaves "fierce wolves will come in among you, not sparing the flock; and from among your own selves will arise men speaking twisted things, to draw away the disciples after them" (vv. 29-30).

Was Paul crazy? He knew that such terrible trouble and false teaching would come, but he was leaving for Jerusalem. How can this be? Didn't he care about the health of the church? If Paul was being run out of the city because of persecution, then we could possibly understand his need to leave, but this was not the case. Even more surprising, Paul knew that he would never see them again (v. 25).

Was Paul being irresponsible? He had been with these disciples for just three years. If these elders were appointed after the first disciples were made in Ephesus, then we can assume they had been elders for less than three years.

If you knew what Paul knew about the future trouble at Ephesus, would you and your team have stayed to help maintain control, or would you have boarded the ship and set sail for Jerusalem "not knowing what will happen" there (v. 22)?

Paul is not being foolish or irresponsible. He is manifesting a missionary faith—something that is seen consistently throughout Acts and Paul's New Testament writings.

Manifesting a missionary faith may be one of the most difficult things your team will be required to do after a church is planted. In order for the Spirit to be in control, your team will have to relinquish control. We often believe that church health is dependent upon us. So we micromanage everything, believing we are more powerful than any potential problem. The irony is that in our attempts to guard the church from problems, we can create problems. The church can become dependent on the team and rely on them rather than on the Spirit, the Word, their elders and one another.

How was Paul able to depart without being unwise or reckless with the church and its leaders? The answer is found in the context of this passage.

- He modeled before the elders (even before their conversion) what it looked like to be a disciple (vv. 18-19).

- He taught them the gospel and the whole counsel of God (vv. 20-21, 26-27).

- He exhorted them to care for both the church and themselves (v. 28).

- He warned them of the problems to come (vv. 29-30).

- He reminded them of his model (vv. 31, 34-35).
- He commended them to God and his Word (v. 32).

Paul manifested a faith in God to do what he said he would do: to sanctify the church and keep it from stumbling and to present it blameless (Eph 5:25-32; Jude 24) before him. Although Paul himself would not return, he would send Timothy to spend time with the church in Ephesus (1 Tim 1:3). He would also write his letter to the Ephesian believers.

Paul's confidence was not in the Ephesian elders or in the training he gave them, nor did his faith rest in the model he provided. Rather, Paul kept his eyes on Christ, who promised to build his church (Mt 16:18). Your team may have little confidence in the new leaders and churches. They are likely to do things differently than your team. But that is not necessarily a bad thing. Your team will probably be pleasantly surprised at their insights and actions as the Spirit leads them in their context. They may seem a little rough around the edges by your cultural standards, but remember: at one time someone probably said the same thing about you.

Fear of what *might* happen can consume you. The only possibility of escaping such fear is to look to the one who loves the new church more than your team does. Do your part in being faithful and imparting wisdom, and do not abandon the new pastors and churches. Manifest missionary faith so that the church and its leaders can run the race they are called to run while your team phases out from the immediate context.

Question: How will these pastors be trained?

Answer: Your team trains them. In fact, everything the team does (even before the people come to faith) involves teaching the people what it means to be a disciple and to make disciples. Your team should decide how you will teach the whole counsel of God to them. Make sure your training is obedience-oriented. It is not enough to provide them with knowledge; you must also hold them accountable to apply the truth to their lives. Right doctrine and right actions should accompany any pastoral training. Your team needs to equip leaders with the right beliefs, passion and skills for their context. Provide them with on-the-job training. Don't create a system that takes them out of the culture while they are trained. Leave them where they are and meet them there. Adjust to their schedules.

Question: When is someone ready to serve as an elder?

Answer: A universal timeline cannot be established for all people. Your team will need to consider this matter prayerfully in light of the sanctification you observe among the people. Obviously, potential pastors must manifest the biblical requirements. Ask yourselves whether they are available to serve in this capacity. Are they willing to make the commitment, not just to serve but to be equipped as well? Do they connect with the people?

Question: What if these elders make mistakes?

Answer: They will. And you will make mistakes too, but that does not necessarily mean that you are disqualified from service. We all make mistakes. Your team should be wise. It should allow the pastors freedom when they begin serving, and serve them as mentors. This means that the new pastors do have freedom but not free rein. There is an art to raising up leaders. Your team will need to discern how much liberty should be provided so that they do not destroy themselves or the church. Remember, Paul was not hesitant to step in and correct problems. We see this throughout his writings. He gave specific instructions to Timothy regarding his ministry in Ephesus with the church and its elders (1 Tim 1:3; 2 Tim 2:2).

Question: Do the pastors need to receive financial compensation from the church to serve?

Answer: No. While a day may come when the church wants to provide them with an honorarium (1 Tim 5:17) or something else, leave that up to the church. That question is up to the self-governing and self-supporting church body.

Question: Is our work finished when the church has elders?

Answer: No. As we saw in the Church Multiplication Cycle, after elders are appointed the team's role becomes that of a developer and then a mentor/partner. The team will have less and less direct influence and presence with the body when they gather and more and more influence and presence with the elders. Your team is now responsible for *necessary* theological and leadership training that is appropriate for the context. Consider putting together an elder development process for a short period of time, allowing for such training to address immediate questions and needs for the new pastors. After this time of equipping, consider using a periodic (for example, monthly) mentor time for accountability, teaching, encouragement and prayer.

Question: Wouldn't it have been better if Paul and his team had contacted the Jerusalem church or the Antioch church to send some pastors to serve the new churches? Elders in those churches were more mature in the faith and more experienced than those in the new churches.

Answer: No. In God's economy for kingdom advancement, there is an *expectation* that pastors will come from the new believers in newly planted churches. They are of the people and from the people. While it is biblically permissible for pastors to come from outside the newly planted churches, this should be the exception in church planting, not the expectation.

SUMMARY

One of the most important developments in the life of a new

church is the appointment of its first pastors. According to Paul, these leaders are a gift to the church for the equipping of the saints:

> And he gave the apostles, the prophets, the evangelists, the shepherds and teachers, to equip the saints for the work of ministry, for building up the body of Christ, until we all attain to the unity of the faith and of the knowledge of the Son of God, to mature manhood, to the measure of the stature of the fullness of Christ, so that we may no longer be children, tossed to and fro by the waves and carried about by every wind of doctrine, by human cunning, by craftiness in deceitful schemes. Rather, speaking the truth in love, we are to grow up in every way into him who is the head, into Christ, from whom the whole body, joined and held together by every joint with which it is equipped, when each part is working properly, makes the body grow so that it builds itself up in love. (Eph 4:11-16)

Shepherds are part of an equipping ministry that facilitates the building up of the body in unity and knowledge. Their ministry assists in the maturation of the church, resulting in (among other things) its protection from deception. It is as this maturation occurs that the church experiences how every member ministers out of a deep love for Christ and one another.

Pastors are necessary. The first leaders are significant for setting the initial course for the church. Working with the church to appoint elders is an important matter. Make sure your team

- does not deviate from the biblical prescriptions;
- is willing to deviate from cultural expectations; and
- manifests missionary faith.

eleven

Strategy Development

•••

"You've just got to be faithful to the Lord. When we get to the field, we'll just be faithful and the Lord will plant his church." This is an extremely important statement for any missionary team. Without faithfulness to the Lord, all is in vain. Apart from him we can do nothing (Jn 15:5).

However, there have been many teams who have used the "faithfulness approach" as an excuse to avoid making any plans. While the Lord demands our faithfulness, he also expects us to use the wisdom, discernment and knowledge of missions he has provided for us over the centuries. To enter the field without a strategy is to plan for failure. And of course, if there is no plan, there is no accountability: if things do not work out on the field, we can just tell ourselves that God must not have wanted to work among these people at this time—after all, we were faithful.

Faithfulness without a strategy is foolishness.

Developing a church-planting strategy is a matter of kingdom stewardship. We rarely travel somewhere without a plan—some means to get to our destination. A strategy serves as a map for a church-planting team as they move through the five steps (see chap. 4) of their work, taking the steps of (1) sharing the gospel, (2) making disciples, (3) starting a small group, (4) planting a church and (5) appointing elders (see fig. 2, chap. 4).

Strategy enables the missionary team to stay focused in their work. It is a prayerfully discerned, Spirit-guided process of preparation, development, implementation and evaluation of the necessary steps involved for church planting.[1] It describes what the team believes the Lord would have them accomplish. (For more information on strategy development and church planting, see chapters nine and ten in *Discovering Church Planting* and *Developing a Strategy for Missions*, pp. 193-263.)

PRAYERFULLY DISCERNED

Throughout every stage on the pathway to planting, the church-planting team must pray, pray, pray. This is especially important when it comes to developing their strategy. God's ways are not our ways, and his thoughts are not our thoughts (Is 55:8-9). As the writer of Proverbs says, "The heart of a man plans his way, but the Lord establishes his steps" (16:9), and "Do you see a man who is wise in his own eyes? There is more hope for a fool than for him" (26:12). The team needs to walk closely with the Lord, seeking both a vision and the means to accomplish it through the church-planting journey. Fasting and prayer should be a regular part of the team members' lives. (For more information on prayer and church planting, see chapter five in *Discovering Church Planting*.)

SPIRIT-GUIDED

The Holy Spirit is dynamic. The Spirit of God reveals the mind of God (1 Cor 2:11). He is actively at work in the world and dwells within all believers (1 Cor 6:19). The Spirit led Philip to the Ethiopian eunuch (Acts 8:29). He led Paul and Silas to Philippi, even though it was not part of their original strategy (Acts 16:6-10).

Strategy development is about walking in step with the Spirit. The team should do nothing to grieve or quench the Spirit in their lives (Eph 4:30; 1 Thess 5:19). Strategic development and implementation is a supremely supernatural endeavor. (For more on the Holy Spirit and church planting, see chapter four in *Discovering Church Planting*.)

PROCESS

Moving through the Church Multiplication Cycle (fig. 5, chap. 7) is a process that involves the preparation, development, implementation and evaluation of the team's plans.

- *Preparation*: Teams must do their homework, both on themselves—how they are shaped as a team—and on the people they are working with—geographically, demographically, culturally, spiritually, historically, politically and linguistically. (For more information on understanding a people and context and questions teams should ask, see chapter twelve in *Discovering Church Planting*.)

- *Development*: Teams must think though the steps they need to take—both major and minor—to move from the pre-entry stage to the church stage.

- *Implementation*: While the team can develop a strategy entirely in a boardroom (this is not recommended), eventually the strategy has to be applied to the field. A strategy is made to be implemented. And with implementation will come ongoing revisions to the strategy as the team evaluates their progress.

- *Re-evaluation*: From start to finish the team must regularly re-evaluate their strategy. This aggressive re-evaluation will help them see necessary midcourse adjustments. The team must always be asking whether they are being wise stewards of the

Lord's resources and whether their strategy is leading to the accomplishment of their original vision.

Much of this process involves asking good questions, responding with healthy answers and applying wise action steps. To help with your strategy development I have included the following questions for you and your team to discuss as you develop your strategy:

- What is the vision your team will work to see realized?

- What are the strengths and limitations of your team?

- Is your team aligned with the vision?

- What resources are available to your team (time, money, people, partnerships and so on)?

- What are your immediate goals (year one), short-range goals (years one to three) and long-range goals (beyond year three) that you must achieve at these three levels before the vision is accomplished? Make sure your goals are measurable and achievable in set amounts of time.

- What methods are you using to accomplish your goals? Are they biblically appropriate? How reproducible are they?

- Are you prepared to make the necessary adjustments as the team works toward seeing the vision accomplished?

- What is your plan to re-evaluate your strategy? Are you willing to aggressively re-evaluate your strategy and methods on a regular basis?

- How is your team held accountable to your church, agency, network or denomination?

SUMMARY

Developing a strategy is crucial for wise kingdom stewards. Though strategies can be developed away from the field to a degree, teams should understand that their strategy will inevitably morph as they enter into the context of the field and engage with the people. What is developed in the boardroom will not stay the same in the field. Wise teams go with a plan but constantly re-evaluate and adjust as they go.

The birth of the Philippian church is a fascinating story related to strategy. Though Paul's missionary team tried to carry out their vision, the Spirit changed their plans (twice!) and led them to a completely new vision in a new direction (Acts 16:6-15). They initially tried to share the gospel in Asia but were forbidden by the Holy Spirit (v. 6). Revising their strategy, they made plans to go to Bithynia, but the Spirit did not allow that either (v. 7). Later, Paul had a vision of a man in the region of Macedonia calling to them (v. 9), so the team concluded that God was calling them there (v. 10).

They decided to start in Philippi, probably because of its influence as an urban center in the district (v. 12). After spending some time in the city, the team ended up at a place of prayer and shared the gospel with some women (vv. 13-14). The first believer was Lydia, not the man from Paul's vision!

Strategy is important, but it must be held loosely. Ongoing re-evaluation and adjustment is imperative. Teams walking in the Spirit should not be surprised when things do not go as planned. Nevertheless, the Spirit often uses our initial plans to redirect us where he wants us to go. It is often when we're planning for Asia and Bithynia that the Spirit leads us to Philippi.

Are you and your team open to this mindset about the Spirit and strategy?

twelve

Ethical Guidelines

•••

I f we say we are kingdom citizens living by a kingdom ethic, then that ethic must govern every part of our lives, including our approaches to church planting. In Christ we have great freedom with our church-planting methods, but that freedom is not unlimited.

Our way of life is the way of Jesus. Just as we have received him, we must continue to walk as he walked (Col 2:6). Since life in the kingdom consists of being a slave and a good steward of the king's resources (Mt 25:14-30; Lk 12:35-48), making most of the time and opportunities (Eph 5:16; Col 4:5) and walking in wisdom (Eph 5:15), *freedom in church-planting practices should only be permitted to the extent that proper stewardship, faithfulness and wisdom are not compromised for some lesser good.* Church-planting practices are ethical reflections of biblical foundations. Poor missionary practices are not just bad methodology; they betray a lack of integrity and a neglect of the moral stewardship proper to a kingdom citizen.[1]

MATTERS OF CONCERN

In the face of great spiritual opposition and the challenges of ministry, church planters often have to fight the temptation to accomplish something *good* for the kingdom at the expense of accomplishing something *great* for the kingdom. Faced with diminishing resources, people who are resistant toward the gospel, and pressures to start a public worship service and to produce certain numbers (either external pressures from supervisors, partnering churches and so on, or internal pressures like insecurity, fear or the desire to prove something), teams can start down a path that deviates from biblically based and missiologically guided church multiplication strategies. This chapter offers a set of guidelines to keep teams properly focused and engaged, especially when challenges come.

ETHICAL GUIDELINES

The following standards of ethical practice in church planting are suggested with the welfare of both the church planters *and* the new churches in mind. These guidelines are a means to assist church planters in their own walk with the Lord. They are written to aid in the church planters' own growth in Christ by keeping a kingdom ethic in place by which they can align their team and work. But these guidelines are also given to help church planters plant churches that are healthy from their birth so that they may present everyone mature in Christ (Col 1:28).

This is not an exhaustive list. You may wish to add your own additional guidelines. All of these guidelines should be adapted to the context and circumstances of your church-planting team.

Guideline 1. Since the global need for the gospel is so great, your team should begin its ministry among people with the greatest need *and* with a high level of receptivity to the gospel *unless God reveals otherwise.*

Following the content of chapter nine, it is generally poor stewardship to begin laboring in areas where there is little need for additional work while there are still four billion people in the world who are not believers and who have little or no access to the gospel. Similarly, unless the Lord specifically leads church planters to a hard soil, church-planting teams should prioritize work among the most receptive. It is unethical to neglect those who are already asking the Philippian jailer's question (Acts 16:30) in favor of people who are cursing the name of Christ.

Guideline 2. Since there are four billion unbelievers in the world, of whom two billion have never even heard the gospel, your strategy should involve the use of highly reproducible church-planting methods.

It is unethical for missionaries to model complex and highly technical methods before new believers and churches, implying that such methods are required for church-planting. This makes it difficult for the new believers to spread the message themselves and to plant churches across their social networks.

Guideline 3. Since biblical church planting is evangelism that results in new churches, your team should not prioritize transfer growth (moving members from one church to another) over conversion growth by designing ministries that will primarily attract long-term kingdom citizens.

Biblical church planting is evangelism that results in new churches. Church planters are missionaries who follow the apostolic paradigm modeled by Jesus and the apostolic church. Though not all transfer growth is bad (for example, if a believer moves into a new city after a job transfer and wants to be a part of a church), it should not be the primary or even secondary concern of your team. Church planting is about making disciples. Church planters should have the desire of the apostle Paul: "to preach the gospel, not where Christ has already been named, lest I build on someone else's foundation" (Rom 15:20).

Church planting is not about attracting a crowd or launching a worship service; rather, it is about the advancement of the kingdom as unbelievers become followers of the living God through local expressions of the body of Christ. Though attracting crowds and starting new worship services are not always bad things, their manifestations do not necessarily mean the kingdom has advanced.

Guideline 4. Since unity among churches in a geographical area is a powerful witness to the gospel, your team should work to maintain open relationships with any other church planters and pastors laboring among the same people group as your team. Your team should take the initiative to meet with them and to share your own ethical guidelines and the definition of biblical church planting. You should emphasize the fact that your team is not there to compete with them.

Jesus prayed that his church would be unified (Jn 17:11, 23) and said that the world would know his disciples by their love for one another (Jn 13:35). A spirit of division, competition, resentment or hostility between believers hinders kingdom expansion and sanctification.

Guideline 5. Since your team's calling to this ministry, people and location is from God and is not based on money, your team should not end your ministry in this area just because your financial support ends. Rather, make appropriate plans (during the pre-entry stage) for the future of your personal finances if your financial support has an expiration date.

Knowing that the sands in the hourglass of income run out quickly for teams not employed in the marketplace, many church planters begin well but decide to shortcut their work when the income dries up. What begins with a focus on making disciples often becomes an exercise in obtaining transfer growth when disciple making takes longer than expected and money is short.

Church-planting teams must develop their strategy in light of the question, "What if our funding ends?" long before any crisis occurs. If the team only has three years of funding, then before they begin their work they must ask the question, "How will we provide for ourselves and our families in three years?" Avoiding the question with the attitude, "God will provide," can be a lack of wisdom masquerading as faith. God will provide—but what if he wants the team members to get jobs in the community? Are the team and the new church ready for the changes in schedule and availability this will bring after three years of "full-time service"? Such changes will require substantial adjustments to the team's daily calendar.

Guideline 6. Since a team approach is the biblical model for church planting, and many liabilities come when working as a solo church planter, it's best to develop your team before the work begins.

Though I am certain that many solo missionaries have planted healthy churches over the years, the solo approach is potentially problematic. It sets church planters up for burnout because they can't divide up the ministry labors. It sets them up for discouragement because they don't have any teammates to provide encouragement. Solo church planters lack accountability. Since intense spiritual warfare is to be expected in such missionary labors, it's wise for church planters to take every precaution to ensure they have the spiritual resources and support at hand to address the warfare when it comes. (For more information on teams and church planting, see chapter fifteen in *Discovering Church Planting* and *The Barnabas Factors: Eight Essential Practices of Church Planting Team Members*, pp. 101-13.)

Guideline 7. Since one of the most critical issues in missionary service is the stress it can put on families, your team should not neglect your families for the sake of church planting but should begin with a strategy for nurturing family life on the field.

There is a widespread perception that missionaries often neglect their families for the sake of the ministry, and certainly there is enough anecdotal evidence to suggest that church planters should be aware of this problem and prepare accordingly. Of all the people who serve the body of Christ, I believe church planters are particularly susceptible to this temptation. Not only do they have the normal pressures of family and ministry, but they are also working to create something from nothing—a daunting task in itself. (For more information on family matters and church planting, see chapter nineteen in *Discovering Church Planting*.)

The church-planting family sets an example of family life for new believers and churches. If the family fails, the ministry will fail even harder. Like the ever-expanding ripples in a calm pond that come when a rock is tossed into the middle, the impact of a family's collapse will extend well beyond the church planter's home, beyond the new believers and beyond the immediate community.

Failure to adequately prepare one's family for church-planting labor or to continually shepherd one's own family suggests that a person is more concerned with accomplishing the task of planting a church than with living according to the kingdom ethic (1 Tim 3:4-5).

Guideline 8. The team should not neglect their daily devotion time with the Lord or allow themselves to be distracted by the numerous tasks of ministry.

The Lord does not need us for his work; he can find someone else if we are unfaithful to him. He desires obedience rather than sacrifice (1 Sam 15:22). One of the great ironies of ministry is that many church planters believe there is so much to do for the Lord that they do not have time to spend with the Lord. They find themselves too busy to pray, to be still and to maintain daily devotions at the feet of Jesus. Whenever the demands of church-planting ministry detract from the church planters' devotion time, an ethical problem crops up. Whenever church planters begin to substitute building the church for spending time with the one who promised to build his church, the ministry is being built on sand.

Guideline 9. Since church planting involves effective communication of the gospel, your team should work diligently toward contextualization, rather than presenting your preferred church traditions to the people as norms. Contextualizing the gospel is always challenging, but some situations are more difficult than others.

One of the temptations church planters face is to practice paternalism rather than contextualization. Paternalism manifests itself as an attitude of superiority instead of humility. Since I have already mentioned paternalism (see chap. 8, "Guidelines for Church-Planting Methodology"), I will move on to the other approach that often takes precedence over contextualization. (For more on contextualization and church planting, see chapter twelve in *Discovering Church Planting*.)

Pragmatism is the philosophy that whatever works is what should be done. All followers of Jesus should be pragmatic to a degree—we are told to make disciples, so we want to know what will work to accomplish this task. But taken too far, pragmatism can become unethical. Church planters eager to see results often do "whatever it takes" to get a church started.

Guideline 10. Your team should report only those numbers and descriptive details that are truly reflective of what the Holy Spirit is doing in your context. Integrity and accuracy are important when reporting statistics related to missionary labors.

Intentionally reporting inaccurate numbers is unethical. It is deceptive and makes God out to be a liar by providing reports that bear false witness against his Spirit. Church planters must always speak the truth (Eph 4:25). The Bible never portrays liars in a favorable light (1 Tim 1:10; 4:2; Tit 1:12).

Though all statistical reporting must be done without reproach, particular care must be taken in reporting numbers related to baptisms and churches planted. An evangelistic gathering is not a church. A Bible study is not a church either, even if it consists of baptized believers. A worship service is not a church. Church planters must not report such groups as churches. Call them Bible studies, seeker studies, seed groups, community groups, preaching points or worship gatherings, but do not call them local churches. Unless the baptized group of believers has self-identified as a church and covenanted to exist and function together as a local expression of the body of Christ, they are not a church. Only after they self-identify should they should be counted as a church—and the moment should be celebrated with much praise and thanksgiving!

Accurate reporting should extend beyond the simple reporting of raw numbers. This is especially important in places that are not highly receptive to the gospel. Church planters should provide a "thick description" of what the Holy Spirit is doing among the people. Stories need to be shared. These stories will encourage both your team and others who read and hear your reports—particularly when the numerical growth is slow. How is the gospel advancing among the people? What ministries are taking place? Who are you praying for? What is the Spirit doing? What conversations are happening? How are things different in the kingdom because of your team's labor among these people?

SUMMARY

Your team should discuss these guidelines (along with any other guidelines you believe should be added to the list). Provide a copy of them to each member and have each individual agree to them. You might even have your team members sign off on them. This is one way to make sure the team is unified in the task. Having a set of guidelines forces the team to discuss a variety of significant issues during the pre-entry stage. Since the ethical guidelines are designed to address major issues, conflicts and disagreements arising from these early discussions are best addressed during team formation instead of on the field, when it is difficult to make major changes.

Conclusion

•••

At the time of this writing, at least four billion people in the world do not have a relationship with Jesus. Many of these are in unreached people groups. They live in remote areas of the Himalayas; they live in your North American town. God has determined when and where people will live (Acts 17:26). He is the divine maestro, orchestrating the movements of the nations on earth that they might find him (Acts 17:27).

Do you see the great need and his hand at work?

He has granted them extensive social networks with family members, friends and acquaintances. These are relational bridges over which the gospel was designed to travel.

Do you see the global possibilities?

He is still calling church-planting teams together (Acts 13:1-3) to cross cultural boundaries to make disciples and plant churches, across the street and across the world.

Is he calling you?

In a world where we have made church planting into something very complicated, the music of apostolic simplicity still plays today.

Do you hear it?

Will you tune your life to it?

The four billion remain.

Acknowledgments

•••

Every book has a story behind its story, which includes a cast of characters who often go overlooked. The author is assumed to be the only person in the story, but that is not the case. Had it not been for the story of the rest of the characters who made the book's story possible, there would never have been a book to read at all.

It has been a wonderful blessing to work with Al Hsu and all of the folks at InterVarsity Press. I am thankful for their professionalism, their love for the Lord and their encouragement to me.

At the time of this writing, I have been serving for almost three years as one of the pastors of The Church at Brook Hills in Birmingham, Alabama. The Lord has blessed me tremendously through these brothers and sisters, whom I love greatly. I also have the honor of serving with an amazing group of elders and staff. I wrote this book with our church members in mind, as we work together to glorify God by making disciples of all nations.

This book would not have been possible without the prayers and support of my immediate family: Sarah, Hannah, Rachel and Joel.

The Lord has been very gracious to me throughout this writing process. I am so thankful for his mercy and guidance. It is my hope and prayer that this book will bring glory to him.

Notes

•••

PREFACE

[1]J. D. Payne, *Discovering Church Planting: An Introduction to the Whats, Whys, and Hows of Global Church Planting* (Downers Grove, IL: InterVarsity Press, 2012).

[2]David J. Hesselgrave, *Planting Churches Cross-Culturally: North America and Beyond* (Grand Rapids, Baker Academic, 2000); Tom A. Steffen, *Passing the Baton: Church Planting That Empowers* (La Habra, CA: Center for Organizational and Ministry Development, 1993); Nathan and Kari Shank, "Four Fields of Kingdom Growth: A Manual for Church Planting Facilitation: Starting and Releasing Healthy Churches," www.movements.net/wp-content/uploads/2012/05/4-Fields-20112.pdf.

[3]Charles Brock, *Indigenous Church Planting: A Practical Journey* (Neosho, MO: Church Growth International, 1994).

CHAPTER 1: WHAT IS CHURCH PLANTING?

[1]Charles Brock, *Indigenous Church Planting: A Practical Journey* (Neosho, MO: Church Growth International, 1994), 30.

CHAPTER 3: PRACTICES OF TEAM MEMBERS

[1]J. D. Payne, *The Barnabas Factors: Eight Essential Practices of Church Planting Team Members* (Smyrna, DE: Missional Press, 2008).

[2]Neil Cole and Robert E. Logan, *Raising Leaders for the Harvest* (St. Charles, IL: Churchsmart Resources, 1995); Steve Smith and Ying Kai, *T4T: A Discipleship Re-Revolution* (Monument, CO: WIGTake Resources, 2011); Robert E. Coleman, *The Master Plan of Evangelism* (Grand Rapids: Flemming H. Revell, 1993).

CHAPTER 4: PATHWAY TO PLANTING

[1]Roland Allen, *Missionary Methods—St. Paul's or Ours?* (Grand Rapids: Eerdmans, 1997), 5.

CHAPTER 5: STAGES OF PLANTING

[1]I am indebted to Tom Steffen and Nathan and Kari Shank for influencing my thinking on these stages. See Tom Steffen, "Selecting a Church Planting Model

That Works," *Missiology* 22, no. 3 (July 1994): 361-76; and Nathan and Kari Shank, "Four Fields of Kingdom Growth: A Manual for Church Planting Facilitation: Starting and Releasing Healthy Churches," www.movements.net/wp-content/uploads/2012/05/4-Fields-20112.pdf.

[2]Nathan and Kari Shank, "Four Fields of Kingdom Growth," 74-78.

[3]Tom A. Steffen, *Passing the Baton: Church Planting That Empowers* (La Habra, CA: Center for Organizational and Ministry Development, 1993).

CHAPTER 6: PLANNED ROLE CHANGES

[1]Nathan and Kari Shank, "Four Fields of Kingdom Growth: A Manual for Church Planting Facilitation: Starting and Releasing Healthy Churches," www.movements.net/wp-content/uploads/2012/05/4-Fields-20112.pdf, 62; George Patterson and Richard Scoggins, *Church Multiplication Guide: The Miracle of Church Reproduction*, rev. ed. (Pasadena, CA: William Carey Library, 2002), 22.

CHAPTER 8: METHODS

[1]Charles Brock, *Indigenous Church Planting: A Practical Journey* (Neosho, MO: Church Growth International, 1994), 89.

CHAPTER 9: WHERE TO BEGIN?

[1]J. D. Payne, *Strangers Next Door: Immigration, Migration and Mission* (Downers Grove, IL: InterVarsity Press, 2012).

[2]J. D. Payne, *Discovering Church Planting: An Introduction to the Whats, Whys, and Hows of Global Church Planting* (Downers Grove, IL: InterVarsity Press, 2012), 161.

[3]John Mark Terry and J. D. Payne, *Developing a Strategy for Missions: A Biblical, Historical, and Cultural Introduction* (Grand Rapids: Baker Academic, 2013), 186-92.

[4]Terry and Payne, *Developing a Strategy for Missions.*

CHAPTER 11: STRATEGY DEVELOPMENT

[1]John Mark Terry and J. D. Payne, *Developing a Strategy for Missions: A Biblical, Historical, and Cultural Introduction* (Grand Rapids: Baker Academic, 2013), 13.

CHAPTER 12: ETHICAL GUIDELINES

[1]Much of this chapter was adapted from my chapter, "Ethical Guidelines for Church Planters: A Suggested Proposal," in Dwight P. Baker and Douglas Hayward, eds., *Serving Jesus with Integrity: Ethics and Accountability in Mission* (Pasadena, CA: William Carey Library, 2010), 225-42. Used with permission.

Bibliography

•••

Allen, Roland. *Missionary Methods: St. Paul's or Ours?* Grand Rapids: Eerdmans, 1962.

Brock, Charles. *Indigenous Church Planting: A Practical Journey.* Neosho, MO: Church Growth International, 1994.

Hesselgrave, David J. *Planting Churches Cross-Culturally: North America and Beyond.* Second edition. Grand Rapids: Baker Academic, 2000.

Patterson, George and Dick Scoggins. *Church Multiplication Guide: The Miracle of Church Reproduction.* Revised edition. Pasadena, CA: William Carey Library, 2002.

Payne, J. D. *Discovering Church Planting: An Introduction to the Whats, Whys, and Hows of Global Church Planting.* Downers Grove, IL: InterVarsity Press, 2009.

———. "Ethical Guidelines for Church Planters: A Suggested Proposal." In *Serving Jesus with Integrity: Ethics and Accountability in Mission,* edited by Dwight P. Baker and Douglas Hayward. Pasadena, CA: William Carey Library, 2010.

———. *Strangers Next Door: Immigration, Migration and Mission.* Downers Grove, IL: InterVarsity Press, 2012.

Shank, Nathan and Kari. "Four Fields of Kingdom Growth: A Manual for Church Planting Facilitation: Starting and Releasing Healthy Churches." www.move ments.net/wp-content/uploads/2012/05/4-Fields-20112.pdf (accessed May 19, 2015).

Smith, Steve with Ying Kai. *T4T: A Discipleship Re-Revolution.* Monument, CO: WigTake Resources, 2011.

Steffen, Tom. *Passing the Baton: Church Planting that Empowers.* La Habra, CA: Center for Organizational and Ministry Development, 1993.

———. "Selecting a Church Planting Model that Works." *Missiology* 22, no. 3 (July 1994): 361-76.

Terry, John Mark and J. D. Payne. *Developing a Strategy for Missions: A Biblical, Historical, and Cultural Introduction.* Grand Rapids: Baker Academic, 2013.

About the Author

J. D. Payne (PhD, The Southern Baptist Theological Seminary) is the pastor of church multiplication at The Church at Brook Hills in Birmingham, Alabama. He is a missiologist and has written several books on mission and evangelism. He previously served with the North American Mission Board of the Southern Baptist Convention and as an associate professor at The Southern Baptist Theological Seminary in Louisville, Kentucky, where he directed the Center for North American Missions and Church Planting. You can find him at his blog (jdpayne.org) and on Twitter (@jd_payne). He lives in Birmingham with his wife, Sarah, and their three children, Hannah, Rachel and Joel.

Other Books by J. D. Payne

● ● ●

The Barnabas Factors: Eight Essential Practices of Church Planting Team Members

Developing a Strategy for Missions: A Biblical, Historical, and Cultural Introduction (coauthored with John Mark Terry)

Discovering Church Planting: An Introduction to the Whats, Whys, and Hows of Global Church Planting

Evangelism: A Biblical Response to Today's Questions

Kingdom Expressions: Trends Influencing the Advancement of the Gospel

Missional House Churches: Reaching Our Communities with the Gospel

Missionary Methods: Research, Reflections, and Realities (coedited with Craig Ott)

Pressure Points: Twelve Global Issues Shaping the Face of the Church

Roland Allen: Pioneer of Spontaneous Expansion

Strangers Next Door: Immigration, Migration and Mission

To the Edge: Reflections on Kingdom Leadership, Mission, and Innovation

● ● ●

Free ebooks available at jdpayne.org:

Unreached Peoples, Least Reached Places: An Untold Story of Lostness in America

Discipleship in Church Planting: Some Guidelines to Move Us Forward

Leading Your Church in Church Planting: Taking the First Steps